D1765641

PARTS OF
SPEECH

One family – three generations of stammerers

First published 2022

Copyright © Tony Millett 2022

The right of Tony Millett to be identified as the author of this work has been
asserted in accordance with the Copyright, Designs & Patents Act 1988.

All rights reserved. No part of this book may be reproduced, stored in a
retrieval system, or transmitted in any form or by any means, electronic,
electrostatic, magnetic tape, mechanical, photocopying, recording or otherwise,
without the written permission of the copyright holder.

Published under licence by Brown Dog Books and
The Self-Publishing Partnership Ltd, 10b Greenway Farm, Bath Rd,
Wick, nr. Bath BS30 5RL

www.selfpublishingpartnership.co.uk

ISBN printed book: 978-1-83952-563-6
ISBN e-book: 978-1-83952-564-3

Cover design by Kevin Rylands
Internal design by Andrew Easton

Printed and bound in the UK

This book is printed on FSC® certified paper

PARTS OF
SPEECH

One family – three generations of stammerers

TONY
MILLETT

Foreword by ED BALLS

'What matters in life is not what happens to you but what you remember and how you remember it.'
Gabriel García Márquez

A quotation that has recently received a slight adjustment:

'What matters in life is not what happens to you but how you tell the story.'

Contents

FOREWORD by Ed Balls

A stammer is like an iceberg, Tony Millett writes in this raw, intense and powerfully uplifting memoir. 'The little bit poking up above the waterline is audible ... the bit that a few people may snigger at ... The much larger part of a stammerer's problem lies hidden well below the iceberg's water line ... all the emotional trappings, fears and forebodings of a stammerer's life.'

In this frank and detailed account of the everyday challenges faced by stammerers, Tony takes us well below the waterline. His lifetime struggle to deal with his own stammer is fully detailed from his pain as a child hearing the stammering King George VI on the wireless, his own fear of swearing a juror's oath in front of the court and the trepidation of speaking his wedding vows in public and then the shocking realisation that his own grandson, Thomas, had inherited the stammer which Tony and his father George struggled with.

Quoting from his diary, written in 1963 when he was just into his early 20s, Tony recalls, 'The sum of the parts was a stammer. It closed me up from the start and set a narrow limit for me.'

And yet, of course, it didn't. *Parts of Speech: one family – three generations of stammerers* details Tony's remarkable and successful career in broadcasting and journalism. He can't quite believe how, with his stammer, he scaled such heights and carried such responsibility in leadership roles at ITN, Channel 4 News and since. But he did – stammer and all. This book, though, is much more than the story of one man's life with a stammer. It is the remarkable story of three generations of stammerers, all members of one family. And while stammering is ever present, this book paints a much broader canvas, chronicling the impact of war on this family and the post-war Britain that followed: death and grief, loneliness and isolation, literature and the flourishing of broadcasting, all form part of this thoughtful meditation.

At the book's heart is Tony's yearning to understand the life and stammer of his father who died a war hero in the months following the D-Day landings in 1944, when his son was just under three years old. 'Like me', Tony writes of his father, 'he had a stammer. I was too young to remember him.' But by reading and quoting extensively from his father's letters home and the powerful tributes sent to George's family by his friends and fellow soldiers, Tony and all of us can take inspiration from what his father managed and conquered in order to be able to lead in battle. 'It helps me get to know a little bit more about my father and the challenges he faced', he writes.

One story stands out in particular, Tony's mother telling him about his father receiving an OBE from fellow stammerer King George at Buckingham Palace in May 1944, just a month before the invasion which took his life. 'As you can imagine,' she chuckles, 'Daddy and the King did not get very far with the usual small talk. They both stammered a lot and

then there was a lot of silence. I think they both just smiled ...'
What bravery they both showed in service to their country.
Tony's depictions of his family's professional soldier, journalist
and student each tell us a great deal about negotiating a stammer,
about changing attitudes to stammering and, more latterly, about
improvements in therapy. It is impossible not to be moved by
Tony's shock when he learns that his grandson Thomas has a
stammer. At times he is tearfully consumed by guilt. But this is
no sob story. Instead, the book ends with a powerful call to arms
and a hugely optimistic view of what the future holds, for Thomas
and coming generations of young stammerers.

Tony details the great progress that Thomas has made with the
inspiration of his granddad, the love of his parents, Susannah and
David, the brilliant work of his speech therapist, Carolyn Wright,
and the hugely influential fortnight-long course that Thomas and his
family took at the Michael Palin Centre for Stammering Children.

This book aims to change how stammering is viewed and
understood, to galvanise more action to support young stammerers
as early as is practicable and to raise the funds to do so, especially for
Action for Stammering Children – the charity that funds and works
with the Michael Palin Centre, and of which I am a Vice-President.

Tony makes his case for better understanding and greater
action on every page. But he does so most powerfully by ending
with words of grandson Thomas as he reflects on what the ASC-
funded Michael Palin Centre course has given him:

'The most valuable thing it gave me was new confidence and a
new way to think about my stammer. It gave me a new perspective
and encouraged being open about having a stammer, and to see it
as a part of who you are, rather than something to be ashamed of.'

Brilliant, accurate and eloquent. How chuffed Thomas' granddad must be. How proud his great-grandfather would be now.

Ed Balls
Vice-President, Action for Stammering Children
August 2022

INTRODUCTION

As any gambler will tell you, two in a row is coincidence. However you calculate or massage the odds, three in a row is a stretch too far. There I was researching my father's life and pondering the nasty coincidence that he and I both lived with lifelong stammers, when a stammer appeared in a third generation of our family. This was no gambler's gift horse. When I retired from full-time work, I thought my stammer no longer really mattered. Occasionally, it might still trip me up, but it would no longer be there at work to raise my anxiety levels and produce that almost fixed level of stress. So I had relaxed a bit. However, this news set me thinking hard about my own stammering experience, and also wondering how my father outdid his stammer to make a successful career in the British army. Above all I wanted to know how in the twenty-first century a bright young grandchild could be helped. How far had treatments and, most importantly, their availability come since my own childhood? How would a young stammerer be treated now – by others and especially by his peers in school? Those first signs of a suspiciously unyielding stammer were like a sucker punch. It sent me reeling. However, as we shall find out in the third part of this book, all was not lost. There was excellent help at hand.

There are some occasions a stammerer simply cannot escape. Those duff days will generally involve having to speak in public. Words aloud – and often not words that can be changed to suit the stammerer. All stammerers have their private thesaurus of alternative words that avoid sounds most likely to trip and block their speech. But for these scary occasions he or she has to take a deep breath and make as best a shot as they can at getting out the fixed words. Long ago, a few weeks after we got our first mortgage and home, I was summoned to jury service for the Quarter Sessions at a nearby District Court. I was scared stiff I would fail to say the juror's oath and be marched from the court. Or on better days, I imagined a fierce judge looking down his nose and saying: 'I am terribly sorry Mr Millett, but I couldn't hear those very important words. Can you please try again – once again – with feeling this time.' I certainly could, but my words would probably not be any clearer to his Lordship's ears.

Standing tall, nervous and already embarrassed, I decided to try a tactical swerve round the most obvious blocking word. The hard 'g' of 'God' was too much of a risk. So I opted to affirm – pointing at the card in the clerk's left hand, the hand that did not hold the Bible. To my horror the words on that card included two hard opening 'd' sounds that brought me to a spluttery halt. 'Declare' and 'defendant' became inaudible as I raced for the end of the oath. Trying to avoid one trap, I had fallen into another. However, no one in the court seemed to mind my garbled oath. It was after lunch so perhaps the judge was a bit too sleepy to mind. But I minded. I minded a lot. It was a bad start to my jury service. Many years later I was called to give evidence at a local magistrates' court. It was a fairly serious motoring case. Once again, though older and supposedly a bit wiser, I was intimidated by the court palaver, and found myself stammering very badly. I do not think I did the prosecution any favours.

Another of those public 'occasions' was a very personal one – very real indeed and certainly not one I could escape. The days before our wedding were full of fear – only, I must add quickly, fear I would not be able to speak my vows. All those names would be nigh on impossible. My forenames would be difficult enough, but my wife's first and second name were going to bring me to another stammering halt. At least I would not be called on to say my surname aloud – that's a hard 'm' I nearly always come unstuck on. Luckily we were to be married by a very calm and sympathetic man, the father of a good university friend. He agreed to say my part of the vows quietly in unison with me – providing the necessary momentum for me and I was fluent for those essential moments – moments I could not allow myself to mess up.

Those were three rather special occasions. The nasty truth is that my stammer never waited to catch me at 'occasions', it was there every day of my life bringing a variety of everyday humiliations – from small to great. It was trying to say my name or give my address, or making a tricky phone call – all parts of another person's normal, everyday life. Some I could brush off relatively quickly, or forget or bury. With year upon year of enforced practise, the smaller problems have become as water off a duck's back. Some others stick firmly in my mind and would leave their mark. I should draw a line now between those passing humiliations and being ashamed of my speech and its lack of fluency. I do not think shame came into it at all.

Stammering is more widespread, more of a universal block on ability than is generally acknowledged. Some statistics from recent research in the United Kingdom – courtesy the charity Action for Stammering Children – underline this. Up to eight per cent of people experience stammering at some point in their lives – thirty-eight per cent of adolescents who stammer have at least one diagnosis of a mental health disorder – up to one and a half million children and young people in the UK can be affected by stammering as they are growing up. Sixty per cent of people who have a stammer have a family member who also stammers – has stammered or still stammers. By a ratio of four-to-one boys are more likely to stammer than girls.

Bucking that statistical imbalance of the sexes, we can note briefly the impact of a stammer on two famous women, two actresses (as they would have liked to be known) from Hollywood's list of greats, whose speech difficulties were, in their lifetimes, unknown to their many fans. In the early decades of the twentieth century we find an American star of the silent screen, who stammered (or as the Americans insist, stuttered). In one dash for freedom Marion Davies had gone from convent school to chorus line, and soon graduated to the famous *Ziegfeld Follies*. At seventeen she was hired for a stage show – with speaking parts. The director discovered she could not speak a stammer-free line and she wound up dressed in the Stars and Stripes singing one song. After her death in 1961, an 'autobiography' was knitted together from hours of tape recordings she had made about her life: 'I couldn't act, but the idea of silent pictures appealed to me, because I couldn't talk either. Silent pictures were right up my alley.' Aged nineteen, she began a partnership with the fifty-three-year-old newspaper magnate William Randolph Hearst that lasted till his death in 1951. She was his mistress, he was her manager – financing her movies and promoting her in his newspapers. By the time she was twenty-seven she had become Hollywood's number one box office draw. All the while none of her fans knew she had a 'persistent stammer'. Why would they? She was an actress in silent movies – loved by the camera and her fans.

Her very lucrative career was put in jeopardy by two events. First, newspapers linked her to a murder. Their link was fallacious and she took them to court. But when she arrived at the crowded court as the main witness, she took fright: 'If you stutter, the implication is that you're guilty – immediately. I got up and ran for the car and went home.' Her case was lost. Then came the first 'talkies': 'There can't be talkies. I'm ruined. I'm wrecked.' Hearst was so alarmed the talkies would sink his financial investment and destroy his lover, that he mounted a doomed campaign to stifle the new talkies. However, Marion fought on: 'I tried talking with a pebble in my mouth, like Demosthenes. It may have worked for Demosthenes, but it didn't for me. I just swallowed the pebble ... Now I had to beat myself into talking.' And she did. In her first talkie – *Marianne* – she could speak some lines with a phoney-French accent. In case of disaster that film was made in both sound and silent versions. But because Marion had found her voice, the silent version stayed firmly in the can.

Marilyn Monroe's rise to stardom came later in the twentieth century, missing the silent movie era. Her stammer started when she was very young, during her time in an orphanage. It soon went away, but came back when she was at secondary school and had to speak publicly in class. Her stammer would reappear at times of stress and mental anguish. It was down to her stammer that she took a record breaking number of takes for a short scene in *Some Like It Hot*. She could not get out the 'sh' sound in her line 'It's me, Sugar'.

We learn little about Marilyn Monroe's stammer from the long list of her biographies. Indeed Norman Mailer in his 1973 90,000 words soup mentions her stammer only once. He muses on the possibility it began when a much-loved dog, Tippy, was shot dead by a neighbour. He then reveals that at one of her foster homes she was called 'The Mouse': 'She would sit and listen, too timid to make a sound ... she could not speak with ease.' Yet Mailer does not attach that – or later speech problems – directly to her stammer. It is almost as though he did not want to believe she could be blighted by something as mundane and disabling as a stammer.

Perhaps it is as well Mr Mailer did not bother to tell us how much Marilyn Monroe fretted before auditions or camera tests, or how terrified she was having to perform in front of acting classes, let alone in front of a Hollywood studio crew prone to bitchiness. Too much reality undermines stardom. She, however, was honest enough to call her experiences of stammering both 'terrible' and 'painful'. She would get round it by adopting, as advised by a speech therapist, her trademark 'breathy speech'.

Some people who stammer can go for years keeping it a virtual secret. It is being required to speak in public that really gives the game away. If King George V's second son Bertie had not had to take over the throne from his elder brother and become King George VI, we might never have known he suffered with such a debilitating stammer.

It was in 2009 that I first realised my experience with a stammer might be of some interest and some use to others. At times of significant work-related stress, I used to go to bed on Saturday afternoons for some recuperative rest. BBC Radio 4 would send me to sleep. One day I woke to hear someone stammering – really quite badly. It was King George VI. In fact, it was Mark Burgess' radio play *A King's Speech*. Within a year we were marvelling at the film *The King's Speech* – scripted by David Seidler who had a stammer he thought had been caused by the traumas of the Second World War and the Holocaust during which his grandparents were murdered. With the resounding success of this film, the media was full of stuff about stammering – and we watched some extraordinary television programmes devoted, in whole or in part, to stammering. For a few weeks I thought that politicians might just catch the spirit of the moment, realise the importance of fluent speech and put money into a proper and full service of Speech And Language Therapies – whose staff, where they exist, are the **SALT** of the earth.

Then came the political decision to impose austerity on our little island corner of the third rock from the sun, and the provision of such essential therapies went backwards. Sadly, quite a long way backwards.

This book is the story of three generations of stammerers: three male members of one family. This not a unique happening – stammering often runs in families. But these three generations extend over more than a century – a period of massive change and improvement in attitudes to stammering and its treatment. Being more open about stammering is wonderful, but it should not hide the fact that stammering still disfigures many lives and, more especially, can stunt many young lives. The story takes my family's stammering through the twentieth century and into the twenty-first. Developments during the last quarter of the twentieth century and the first years of the present century, have delivered great changes in the available treatments for stammers. Though it is still important to realise that stammers are rarely – if ever – cured absolutely. Stammerers can be helped and taught how to overcome their stammers to a degree that dysfluency in their speech is seldom noticeable. I cannot repeat too often that openness about stammering is an essential launch pad for progress in ending its often tyrannous reign.

I will describe many everyday ways a stammer can affect a person's life, can limit their opportunities (the stammerers' equivalent of the 'glass ceiling') and skew life-altering decisions – especially when early speech therapy is not appropriate or doesn't work or is simply not available. Not all stammers and not all stammerers are the same – of course they are not. So the experiences in these pages are just examples.

The news about our grandson brought back with a terrible jolt a statistic that had long lurked at the back of my mind, but which I had never expected to apply to future generations of our family: forty per cent of those in the United States who stammer have inherited their disability. More recently the proportion of inherited stammers identified by scientists has been revised upwards to 'nearly half'. Our family have become part of that statistic – with stammers of varying intensity inherited over three generations. We are now finding out that our DNA is much more complex than we gathered from those early newspaper headlines welcoming the discovery of the gene that governs in-growing toenails – or whatever.

I need to take a leaf from that excellent scientist, writer and broadcaster Adam Rutherford – from his must read book *How to Argue with a Racist*:

> 'Nature – meaning DNA – has never been *versus* nurture – meaning everything that isn't DNA. ... Nurture – meaning the non-genetic environment – does not mean whether your parents cuddled you or ignored you as a child; it means every interaction between the universe and your cells, including how you were raised, but also everything from the orientation of you as *foetus in utero*, to the randomness of happenstance, chance and noise in a very messy system.'

With that clarification of the age-old nature/nurture battles in mind and despite the firm intention that this is not an autobiography, I may, from time to time, veer away from the task I have set for this memoir and venture into personal moments that readers think they do not need to know about. It will just be me attempting to fill in the nurture bits – what I am calling (courtesy Dr Rutherford) the 'messy' bits. They – with their little nudges and bigger traumas – steer our lives in more ways than the stuff we inherit. Messy jeans taking on messy genes. Somewhere in my genes there was this predisposition (is 'susceptibility' a better word for it?) for a stammer to develop. It was probably triggered by a specific bit of this 'mess'. As this memoir unfolds, we may find out what that bit of 'mess' was.

I am not sure whether it would be possible or worthwhile trying to write a book about a stammer without a pretty full picture of the people whose first-hand experience is being produced in evidence. Character and stammer are so intimately connected. We may, therefore, also delve into various less obvious autobiographical areas of the two older members of this trio.

Before we set off on this journey, I should make it quite clear that the larger and best part of my stammering life would not, could not have happened as it did without Alison. We married in 1966 and she has been my essential support ever since. Words of deep appreciation and thanks to her are never, ever enough. The poet and English Literature scholar Professor Vivian de Sola Pinto (whom I will soon have the pleasure of introducing you to) wrote these lovely lines:

As I sat at my old desk, writing
in golden evening sunshine,
my wife came in suddenly
and, standing beside me,
said, 'I love you'
(this year she will be sixty-three and I shall be sixty-eight)

Then I looked at her and saw
not the grey-haired woman but the girl I married in 1922:
poetry shining through that faithful prose,
a fresh flower in bloom.
I said. 'You are a rose'
(Thinking how awful it would have been if I had missed her)
and I kissed her.

We are now much older than Prof Vivian and his wife Irène were then, but that last parenthesis haunts me daily.

I have had many days and weeks when I thought my stammer

was a disability, other days and weeks when it was just an impediment and many days and weeks when it was barely even a nuisance. There were plenty of good times. They were most often not public times, but times with people who understood and with people whom I cared about and who cared about me. When very young I once heard my stammer referred to as a 'disorder'. This confused me as I thought I always tried to say the words in their right order. For once my stammer gives me a smile.

Besides the obvious problems we have already glimpsed, and the set-piece occasions that caused hesitations and worse, what I really minded was the way my stammer interfered with everyday life: conversations not initiated, names not asked and the small talk that can lead to friendship simply not exchanged. So many paths not taken – and all because of the stammer. But I must add that this book is not written as a lengthy whinge. I have inherited my mother's aversion to martyrs. I don't know how she felt about the Holy Martyrs, but she was very hard indeed on people who made much, often much too much, of an illness or misfortune. So I tread warily.

Until recently, very few people have asked me about my stammer – or talked about stammering at all. This means you have no idea if the person you are talking to is frightened/embarrassed to ask you a question because they may trigger a stammering response, or she/he is frightened/embarrassed you know they are frightened/embarrassed about your stammer. Sometimes silence is the best option.

For many, *The King's Speech* was an eye-opening movie. Prince Charles made a good point when he was launching an appeal for Action for Stammering Children in 2010. He said he was acting as patron of the appeal in memory of his grandfather, King George VI:

'His stammer cut him off I think in so many ways from his parents and his brothers and sisters and drove him into himself as I suspect so many sufferers will understand. Above all he experienced that awful fear of feeling different from others.'

I do, of course, realise that attitudes to disabilities, conditions, differences and spectrums have improved since the 1950s, 1960s and 1970s. I am enormously cheered by those changes. Although they have not improved in all respects. People still need to understand how a stammer can alter young lives and alter behaviour – and need to be taught to accept a stammer as part of each individual and not something to ridicule or joke about. Adults need to be aware that if they feel embarrassed by a young stammerer, it will be as nothing compared to the embarrassment the stammerer is almost certainly feeling.

I have written this book with two prime aims. First, this memoir is political. Relax: it is not about big-P Politics or the 'Westminster bubble'. Its aim is to encourage people at all levels (that's all of us) to support and encourage action on stammering – most especially to help stammering children. It is sickening to find that 'speech and language' therapy services have not survived the austerity decade intact. On the other hand, it is heartening to find there are outstanding centres – including charities – where stammerers are helped and supported successfully. Secondly, I want to use this book to raise funds for one of those outstanding centres: the London-based charity Action for Stammering Children (ASC) at the Michael Palin Centre. Later I shall explain why.

We talk often – and often rather glibly – about 'free speech'.

We should all care more about those who every day face challenges because their speech is not 'free' or not, in the jargon, 'fluent'. Above all, it is ever more vitally important to provide suitable treatment and support for children as soon as their stammer appears.

———————————
———————————

Author's note: Much of my father's story comes via the letters he wrote to his wife before and during the Second World War. I have also used some supporting documents my mother kept, the letters she received after his death, relevant files in the National Archives, and his official army record. Otherwise, I have hunted through a number of histories and biographies and spoken (some years ago) to army veterans who knew my father. [In the text, indented extracts without quotation marks are all from my father's letters.]

PART ONE

1.

LIKE FATHER, LIKE SON – I

There is a photograph of our elder grandson, Thomas, striding through the long grass on the Marlborough Downs. He is aged between three and four and is wearing a very fine pair of coloured wellies. He has a determined look that says he will, come what may, not fall behind the grown-ups and their long legs. It sticks in my mind because, even at that age, he shows the kind of determination that can overcome adversity. Even the most excellent speech therapy can come a cropper if the recipient lacks determination. I just want to mark that image of determination as I start the story of my stammer and its not very determined owner.

———————————

The first documentary evidence that I was developing a stammer comes in a letter my father wrote home on 20 January 1944. He was then based in London working with the British army's 1 Corps on the top secret planning that would eventually end the war in Europe: the invasion of Nazi-occupied France or D-Day or the long-awaited 'second front'. His letter refers to me by my very early nickname – I am not sure he ever accepted Anthony was a suitable name for me. Perhaps the sounds in 'Anthony' could make his speech stick – as sometimes they still do for me:

> Disturbing about A.J.'s stammer. He anyhow shows no indication of being left handed that I've seen. However as we are alive to it, it may be possible to prevent it ...

Unfortunately, that is all of this particular and important letter that survives. After it had been read by my mother, the back of the final page was probably used for her next shopping list. The emphasis on not being left handed came from the widely held belief that stammering was often caused when a child was prevented from being naturally left handed and was made to become right handed – causing some kind of shock or trauma to the 'wiring' in the brain.

After that very early alarm, for several months there was no further mention of my stammer in his letters. I assume my mother, Rita, did not want to worry him while he was working such long hours in London and travelling widely. I do imagine my parents discussing my stammer at length whenever they spoke by telephone and met during his few short weekends on leave at home. Then, after D-Day, he was on very active service – as the War Office put it, 'in North West Europe'.

My stammer did, of course, become much more obvious when I started to talk in sentences. Then my mother really needed his advice and help. So nine months after that first mention, she had written to him with renewed concerns about my stammer. He responded in his letter written on 24 September 1944. He was then commanding an infantry battalion which had come north from Normandy into Belgium, and crossed – after a bloody battle – into eastern Holland, close to the German border. In that day's letter he wrote:

> I am so sorry, darling, about A.J.'s stammer. But as we are alive to it and there are such good experts nowadays if we start at the time he's really beginning to talk I am sure there's a chance of nipping it in the bud. Shall look forward to hearing what the doc says.

On 24 September 1944 I was aged two years and seven months. My father, a professional soldier, was aged forty-one years and five months. Less than three months after he wrote that letter home – one of a constant stream since he had landed in France – he was killed in Holland. On the banks of the River Maas. He was commanding the 2nd Battalion of the King's Shropshire Light Infantry (2 KSLI). The date: 20 December 1944.

Although I cannot remember when I first knew about my father's stammer, I have for very many years assumed mine was inherited from him. That figure stuck in my mind: forty per cent of stammers are inherited. Some people say stammers can be copied – from parents or close family friends. I can hardly have copied my father's speech impediment because, by the time I started talking, I had only been with him for a matter of days. I am a war-baby – born in Salisbury, Wiltshire on 21 February 1942. My father, George Millett, was stationed there as a senior staff officer with Southern Command – helping to defend a large swathe of

southern England against Hitler's intended invasion. We were a
family of four there – Rita, George, Andrew (their firstborn son)
and Anthony (me) – for only a few weeks.

I am being very wary of memories. Some can so easily turn out
to be erroneous or exaggerated. For many years I was certain I did
remember my father – a brief sighting of him walking through
the gates to our house on his way home from the pub at the end
of lane. Then to my disappointment I realised this was a phoney
memory – built round something my mother once told me. It
could not be true as I was picturing the gates to the wrong house.

So this is Dr Rutherford's 'messy' world. We all live in it.
We are surrounded by mess and by clutter. Some of the angst of
my early years was purely caused by the lack of a father and the
decidedly awkward situation my mother was landed in. Once the
glow from the letters of condolence wore off and the disruption
had eased, life was still very tough on a war widow's pension. At
home, my father was hardly ever mentioned. My mother's aim
was not to look back, but to move forward. She had the cares on
her shoulders of a single mother with two sons. She took casual
work to help with the bills. Apart from a very few exceptions, she
was not keen to keep up with army friends. There was, though she
only spoke to me about it much, much later, the feeling that a war
widow of her age could be seen as a target for a second marriage.
Even before she admitted those fears to me, I was well aware of
one army widower with two teenage children, who, shall we say,
'set his cap' – and was told by her in no uncertain terms to leave
her well alone.

At a very young age I confess to finding the war – and my
father's absence – confusing and unsettling. My endless questions

– distressing as I now see many of them were to my mother – grew hazy when she told me the Americans were sending back my father's 'things' – or, in adult language, 'effects'. Why the Americans? I think I was three-plus years old; this event is certainly one of my earliest memories. Two tall men in overalls are bringing something off a lorry. I learned that it looked like the coal man's lorry – only much cleaner. They carry it down the short drive into the garage that stood back from the house we had recently moved into. It was a wooden box – about the size to take a croquet set – made of surprisingly good wood: 'It's mahogany – I'm sure it is', Aunt Nicie said later. But the lid was roughly fashioned from altogether less worthy wood. Looking back I do wonder whether this box, not by any reckoning British army standard issue, had been 'liberated' from some ruined home in Holland. The men put down the box on the rough concrete floor. They say firmly that 'in the circumstances' there is no need to sign for it, and leave hurriedly.

I was not there when the box arrived, but I do recall my mother explaining how it came to be on the garage floor – still unopened. I think I had spent the morning playing next door – out of the way of this troublesome delivery. Later we stood beside it: my mother, her unmarried sister who was Aunt Nicie (or Nice, who would become a major influence on my life) and myself (my elder brother, Andrew, was away at school).

I think it was my aunt who unscrewed the lid of the box to reveal my father's 'things'. On top lay a neatly folded uniform. I do not recall saying anything as the contents were revealed. Perhaps I was going through one of my silent phases – in those days children went through a lot of 'phases'. Or perhaps I was having a bad day's stammering. Three 'things' that appealed to a young boy are uppermost in my memories of that day. First there was a staff officer's slide rule with which you could measure the length and speed of a convoy of trucks. Secondly, a gauge with a little wheel that measured distances on a map. And thirdly, a whacking great torch. It was over a foot – an adult's foot – long. The metal case was a dull colour – much like my father's pewter beer mugs. The top unscrewed to take a number of very fat batteries. But the real interest for me was its legs. It had three neatly shaped legs about an inch and a bit long. These screwed into recessed holes around the lens. The idea was that you stood the torch on its legs over a map. It would illuminate a small circle of map – without giving enough light to reveal your whereabouts. I played with it often. I do remember feeling it was something that my father had used and touched.

My aunt went home to give her mother some supper. My mother retired to bed with an incipient migraine. And I went for a delayed after lunch 'rest'. Some days later the uniform was given away to a man in the village who needed 'working clothes', and the residue of an abruptly ended military life was put into a Gladstone-type bag and stored in the walk-in wardrobe in my bedroom. The empty box stayed in the garage and was once used to store our home-grown potatoes.

That evening, the arrival of the box had at last begun the process of sorting out in my head whose side I ought to be on – *we* ought to be on. At bedtime my mother said: 'How nice of the Americans to send Daddy's things home.' She made no mention of what was in the box. 'Americans – I see,' I replied. 'Yes, how very kind of them.' As the light clicked off in my bedroom, an hour of turmoil began. So little had been said about Daddy and the war that I was even confused as to which side he had been on. Until the arrival of the box, courtesy of the Americans, I had honestly thought the Americans had killed my father. Now I was learning differently. The problem was that I never wanted or dared to ask my mother such basic questions. Partly it was the stammer. Partly it was my fear of her dissolving into tears.

There had, I now know, been an earlier delivery of my father's belongs. These were small items listed as 'Articles of Personal Effects of Intrinsic and Sentimental Value'. They had arrived earlier by post and I was not shown them. I discovered them later when I started to investigate 'Daddy's drawer' in the little chest in the sitting room. With them was the list that came with them – typed in Holland by an army orderly. The parcel had included 'six pipes (1 broken)', postage stamps to the value of 7½d, some photos, a book token, a compass, a Division badge, one 'cheque book (Lloyds)' with 'Nos. 150205-240 unused', a membership card, two propelling pencils, two books and nine keys on a ring.

However silent we were about my father, reminders of him kept turning up. Some months later, another delivery came with the morning post leaving my mother quite disorientated. After the wooden box came a tiny cardboard box. It was utility brown, very rigid with reinforced corners and marked with a black crown within a circle. She opened it with me there, peering over her shoulder. Inside were the medals and ribbons my father had won – or earned. I had no idea what they signified. My mother became very quiet fingering the medals. Then she put them back in the box and brought out from under the folded paperwork a tiny oak leaf in a dull brown metal: 'This is the important one. See, it's a little oak leaf – this is for being "Mentioned in Dispatches" – and it's the most important one of all.' Nothing about how or why it meant so much. Back it went into the box.

Even at a very young age, I was irritated by the silence about my father and about his death. I was once taken out to lunch in London by my uncle – my father's brother. He never talked to me about his brother. As we walked back to the station, he hailed a man on opposite the pavement. What an extraordinary coincidence. This man had once been my father's batman. Ignored, I was left standing apart from them as they chatted away and was never introduced to this man who was a direct connection to my father and might have helped me form a picture of him. Perhaps my uncle was simply trying to protect me from a stammering crisis. Or would he be embarrassed by my stammer? Did he not realise that my father's former batman would have been perfectly well aware of a stammer in the family?

Another indication of the near total silence at home regarding my father's death came in 1950, when my mother took Granny to the Isle of Wight for a short respite stay by the sea. There, by chance, they met a Dutch family and discovered a strange coincidence. Many years earlier, the wife – M. de Bruijn-van Doessburg – had been at the same cookery school as my mother. She promised my mother she would go to Venray cemetery where my father is buried and photograph the grave. Four years later a letter arrived from this lady with four 'snaps' (as she called them) of the cemetery and the grave: 'The cemetery is situated in a nice quiet place. Beautifully kept in order with plenty of flowers.' She apologised for the quality of the 'snaps' saying it had been a very dark day. And she apologised for the four-year delay: 'I am sorry I could not write to you before, but Venray is a long way from our house – about 75 miles.'

I remember my mother opening the letter. She barely looked at the 'snaps' or read the letter, and straightaway put the envelope into a small drawer in her desk where it stayed till she died. I am as certain as I can be that she never looked at it again or showed it to anyone. She certainly never visited his grave. However, when I looked in the envelope the other day, I discovered there were four of the Dutch lady's black-and-white 'snaps' and one other very different looking black-and-white photo – a tiny contact print. This one had the name of the cemetery on the back in my mother's handwriting. I had never seen this photo before. It showed part of the cemetery in wartime before the War Grave Commission installed their iconic headstones and took their inimitable care in layout and landscaping. This tiny photo, printed slightly on the slant, shows a plain wooden cross with black, lettering in a stencilled font. On the cross piece it reads LT/COL. MILLETT CG – 2KSLI/DCLI, and on the upright is his Service Number (25112) and 'K.A. 201244' – Killed in Action 20 December 1944. That it is fairly underexposed makes the white of this cross stand out against the background. It had probably come in January 1945 with a letter of condolence from a member of his battalion.

I had nightmares. Once awake, in the very early still dark mornings, I often lay for hours wondering why this had all happened to me. I sort of knew I would never see him. But being – at that time at least – fully embedded, as it were, in the Church of England, I worried endlessly that I would never catch up with him. When I got to heaven, he would just have been moved on to some other far-off place. I would miss him again. In addition, I found not a jot of consolation in the way the church remembered my father. In the parish church, we always sat in a pew near the front and on the right hand side of the aisle. Directly in front of us was the war memorial listing those men from the village who had been killed in the war. I stared at his name in gilt letters on brown wood – as bible readings slid into sermon – hoping, I think, it would help soften my father's absence. It did no such thing.

My very early stammering years have mostly slipped from my memory. I do not recall having any serious problems with my speech during my year at the village school. I do remember very clearly the whole class chanting together as we counted from one to a hundred. The chanting enabled me to join in fluently. This happened at the end of each day. We started the count at five-to-three. We were allowed to run out into the playground to a waiting parent as the 'big hand reached the top' and it was, at last, three o'clock.

However, I do recall that talking to adults had become something of a gamble. It was not as simple as 'heads-or-tails' and nothing like the straightforward thirty-seven numbers on my toy roulette wheel. I played with it almost daily until the little silver ball flew off who knows where and was lost. Nor was it as simple as settling on one of the twenty-six letters of the alphabet. It was about the multitude of combinations that turned those twenty-six letters into sounds – some I could say without stammering, most I could not say easily, and some proved virtually impossible. The problem was I never knew what adults were going to ask me or talk to me about. The easiest option was simply to make myself scarce so I would not have to speak to adults at all.

I've recently found a typed page headed '*Some Eight Hundred*

Words of Autobiography'. It must date from about 1963 – it was typed on the portable typewriter Andrew gave me for my twenty-first birthday. A sort of diary entry, it makes grim reading – almost certainly written in the bleak and anxious days I spent looking for my first job:

> 'The sum of the parts was a stammer. It closed me up from the start and set a narrow limit for me. It turned me in with rounded foetus-like shoulders and bitten nails.'

I must emphasise that reporting this helps me explain my stammer – it is certainly not a cry for sympathy.

Memory only brings to mind a few instances of the stammer intruding during the three terms I spent at the next school, a day school in a nearby town. The main memory is my inability to learn my tables. I just wonder how far that was influenced by my fear of being told to declaim the 'seven times table' or to answer quickly what seven nines are. First hand up earns the kudos. If I put my hand up and was called, would I get stuck? If so the teacher would ask the next hissing child with a stretched arm and waving hand – 'Me Miss ... please Miss ... I know'. In the 'Eight Hundred Words' I called this school 'rowdy' and explained that it was there I 'discovered gangs and girls teeth – the ones that bite rather than love'. Cripes.

In his letters from France and Holland, my father refers to my 'sunny temperament', my 'crashing form'. Responding to reports in my mother's letters to him, he says that I 'sound great fun' and 'A.J. sounds altogether too intelligent and savvy'. Then all of a sudden the mood music darkens. He wrote in July 1944: 'I am so sorry darling, A.J. has started being silly ...' And ten days later:

'Do hope all goes well with you. A.J. not too contrary and cross – more his good self.' My father would not have been very pleased with my progress – or lack of it. For some years, the sun set on my temperament. I know I showed a distinct lack of confidence, general crossness and was said to be slow to read. So, on Tuesday, 16 November 1948, aged six years and eight months, I was taken by my mother to see a psychologist. I cannot remember whether any specific episode led to this appointment.

That summer the three of us had been to Ireland to stay with an old friend of my mother, the friend's much older husband and their five daughters. I do not remember being particularly awkward during this amazing adventure. I do remember howling when we had to leave. The reason? I had become very attached, very close to, even besotted with, one of the daughters who was barely older than I was. Lovely Maggie, a blonde delight, took me for rides in the donkey cart, played in the hayloft and introduced me to cigarettes (well, *a* cigarette – a poor bent thing extracted a bit shyly from the back pocket of Maggie's junior dungarees). She became expert at finishing words for me – always with a sweet smile. It was in Ireland this war-baby first tasted cream, lots of it. I immediately retired to bed with a very bad tummy. I hope Maggie came to see whether I was getting better.

By November we were well and truly back in the land without cream. My mother and I went by train to The National Association for Mental Health in London, where I had an intelligence test and 'interview' with psychologist Norah Gibbs. Her report revealed I had a mental age of eight years and eight months, and an IQ of 130. I was right-handed and left-eyed and showed '... all the usual signs of poor scholastic attainment connected with this difficulty.'

I like her word 'difficulty', though she did not apply it to my stammer:

'Anthony stammered very little indeed during this interview; he was less able to control his speech mechanisms when he was feeling inadequate in general ... As speech therapy is difficult to arrange locally, I think it would be better for a time to attack the other reasons for lack of confidence, and then review the difficulty in six months' time. He was a most delightful boy to interview.'

I do not think that gave my mother much comfort – however 'delightful' I had been at the interview. Though she was undoubtedly pleased that my IQ level meant I would be '... potentially able to profit by higher education'.

2.

VERY UNWILLINGLY TO SCHOOL

There is one thing I am certain about concerning my first boarding school: I faced it with a total lack of cheerfulness and equanimity. I loathed the idea. Who would finish my words for me? What, for heaven's sake, would be happening at home without me? Who would feed the two hens? Would my mother just retire to bed with her awful-to-watch headaches? Would they turn into migraines? Who would sit beside her in church? Who would look after her? After all, fierce Granny had told me it was my 'job to look after your Mother'.

Despite the fact that I failed for many years to learn my alphabet (after all, I did have to try and say it aloud in class), I actually began to read quite early. This was reading to myself and not, of course, reading aloud. So perhaps failing to read aloud in class led to the idea that I was slow to read. The first real and proper book I read – 'Mummy, I've finished it!' – was *I Sailed with Christopher Columbus*. Sometime before I went off to board at a school two-and-a-half miles from the safety of our home, I got hold of a story by (I am pretty certain) Sapper. Perhaps it came in one of the issues of *Reader's Digest* that the nice old lady next door passed on to me. The bit I remember so clearly tells of a war widow giving a party at her empty home so she could meet new friends (or perhaps meet 'a special new friend' – the world was still in full euphemistic mode). As she takes round a bottle of something (perhaps Dry Fly sherry, my mother's favourite) or a bowl of cheese straws (something my mother enjoyed baking), she looks out through the French windows and sees her supposedly Killed in Action husband walking across the lawn. Surprises could happen. Our home had French windows and a good patch of green lawn ...

For a seeming eternity, boarding school loomed. Absence from home was far from being the worst fears I had about it. First there was the inevitable explaining to goodness how many teachers and fellow pupils why I had no father. What would I say when school friends – steeped in the 1950s glut of war books – asked how he died? Would they believe me if I simply said: 'I don't really know.' Secondly and probably more pressing, my mother had carefully explained to me that I would be called simply by our surname. In some dread I wondered how many times teachers would ask me my name. 'Millett' was – and still is – a trip word for me. I could say 'mustard' with ease. I could say 'mine' or 'mirth' with little worry. But the tight 'm' followed by the very short 'i' defeats me almost every time. It is the same with 'minutes', although I have now learnt to elide the end of the numeral into the 'm' – so it becomes 'sixmin-itts'.

It was in that mood of terrified apprehension that a pre-school disaster occurred. We – my mother and I – went to London to buy school uniform from Messrs Gorringe on Buckingham Palace Road. The approved everyday sweater had a collar that tickled the back of my neck. The blazer had sleeves 'to grow into'. The black 'tie-ups' – shoes for Sundays – pinched my heels. The name-tapes? 'Oh, fourteen days, madam.'

So far not quite the exciting day out that was promised. But it was the man who served us that spoilt it completely. He walked almost on tiptoe and had hair that looked remarkably like the toy drummer boy I had finished with long ago – a drummer boy with centre parted, flat to the scalp hair. At least the shop assistant did not sport – not at least in public – the drummer boy's ruby reddened cheeks. 'What, young sir, have you been up to in the holidays?' No reply. 'Are you going to be enjoying all that geography and history at school?' No reply. 'Or perhaps algebra?' No reply. He looked to my mother for help and then said: 'Has the cat got his tongue today?' Meltdown.

I had lots of answers to his questionable questions, but could not risk a stammering start to a reply, not in public with all those other parents and about-to-be schoolboys around us. I was still young enough to have a good old fashioned, Buckingham Palace Road sized meltdown – all due to the stammer. Stupid man.

In that 'Eight Hundred Words' scrap of paper I summed the prep school up as 'sombre, stoned, religious, over-ruled'. Oh well – those words get more interesting as they move on to shed some light on what I faced:

'For five years I soaked up geography as taught to the Victorians and a gentlemanly training: doors are for going through last, shoes to be cleaned regularly (by someone else, as it happened), shoulders held straight and Mr Green the gardener to be called Green. They split us into squads to instil the competitive and community spirits with one easy imperial move. I was in 'India' and marched behind a flag three years extinct. The dormitories were named after old boys killed in the recent war. I didn't enjoy it. I stammered, was shy, withdrawn and read a lot.'

A brief sketch, recollected not in tranquillity, but apparently in some anger, perhaps during a fit of depression about the stammer. I have only found the first page and it finishes: 'Cures [for the stammer] went on. I gave irrelevant samples to hospitals repeated times ...'

It was, however, about midway through my time at this school that I first realised how much my life was being hemmed in and constrained by my stammer. I began to feel trapped by it. Prior to this slow-burn awakening to reality, I think I had just crashed on regardless. I probably never said all I wanted to say – either at home or at school. But until that bulb flickered alight I suppose I simply had not minded being unable to speak as I wished. I was pretty silent even when playing with or going for walks with the girl next door – with whom I shared secrets such as birds' nests and other parts of our natural life. Diana and her family were very active Chapel-goers. Even aged nine or so, Diana-of-the-lovely-eyes did not think holding hands was okay.

At one end of term assembly, the headmaster produced from *The Times* a difficult general knowledge quiz. I actually knew five or six answers – but I kept schtum. No wonder school reports told my mother I was well behind most of the class. A similar problem was that I could never join in with the endless rounds of joke telling. And jokes were second only to the still-rationed sweets as schoolboys' currency of choice. Did other boys ever tease me about my stammer? Some did, but not many. In the first years at this school, I may have fended off the teasers by being very easily brought to tears – and tears signalled to staff members that something bad had happened, so questions would be asked as to why I was crying. Certainly, it was during the last three years at prep school that my stammer proved to be a real stumbling block. The most memorable disasters I encountered were the annual poetry recital competitions. Each form learnt a poem and one by one its members stood in front of the assembled school to recite it. At the back of the hall sat the headmaster and a local worthy or parent with the unenviable task of sitting through this ordeal by poetry and judging the contest. For me it was utterly daunting.

I can recall three of the poems we had to learn. All three were by Rudyard Kipling: *The Glory of the Garden*, *The River's Tale* ('Twenty bridges from Tower to Kew wanted to know what the river knew ...') and *Merrow Down*, which had first appeared in the *Just So Stories* ('There runs a road by Merrow Down, a grassy track it is today ...'). Despite his helpful rhythm, as soon as I stood at front of the hall, I started to stammer – badly. Strangely, this experience did not put me off poetry. However, ever since those wretched competitions, I have been unable to learn poetry by heart.

The teaching at this school relied on two techniques – reading aloud round the class and endless précis writing. The latter probably prepared me pretty well for a career in journalism. The former was, I suspect, a cheap and easy way to cover the curriculum without much effort on behalf of the teacher. Unsurprisingly I loathed it. Reading round the class was simply terrifying. One subject very prone to frequent lessons devoted entirely to reading aloud was 'Divinity'. I used to try and work out which verse of the Old or New Testament I would get – counting boys ahead of me against verses as they were read. Yet so often some stupid boy read two verses by mistake and my silent practise went for a burton. With Shakespeare it was far worse. You never knew when the teacher would ask a reader to stop and call for the boy in the next desk to take over. Boys in my form would sometimes tease me: 'Let's see if we can get him to read the shortest verse – he should manage that OK.' Had they thought for a second they would have realised that 'wept' did not begin with one of my easy sounds. Anyway 'Jesus wept' is in St John's Gospel which was a bit too abstract for small boys – all that talk of 'the Word'. I certainly stammered my way through several of Shakespeare's most moving and famous speeches, and got well and truly tangled in Moses with his kith and kin and his bulrushes.

Adding to the terror of 'reading round the class', one teacher really angered me. When it was my turn to start reading aloud a poem or a Shakespearean speech, he would glance at his watch and smile conspiratorially at the swots in the front row – as though he was going to time me or was wondering whether I could I get through it before the bell went for the end of the lesson. Did he think he was doing the right thing – defusing an embarrassing situation? He got it very wrong. I hated him.

There was another master at this school who gave me trouble. He was much older than most of the other teachers. He had been at the school for years and years – well before it had to move from the south coast during the war. He really was from another era. Out of school he was caring and generous. During school holidays, he used to take groups of boys on historical sightseeing tours of London. These started with lunch in Ye Olde Cheshire Cheese. Its superior pie and mash was often talked about at school when we faced one of cook's watery and gristly stews.

When it came to teaching his character changed. He reverted to pre-war – even Edwardian – methods of teaching, and to pre-war – even Victorian – methods of discipline. He gave no quarter to any boy who was not keeping up with his rattling pace. He brought into class a rolled-up canvas 'blackboard' on which, in his terribly crabbed handwriting, he had chalked screeds of clauses and phrases for us to parse. Whether it was embarrassment at having to listen to me stammer or his need to maintain his lessons' fierce pace, he totally ignored me. This got so annoying, so infuriating that I complained about him to my mother. She went, reluctantly, she told me, but in the end boldly, to confront the headmaster. He explained how difficult it was for him as this teacher was not only many years his senior, but was also his godfather! Whether he ever did explain to his godfather that I would like the chance to answer an occasional question in a subject area that I thought I was quite up to speed on, I shall never know. However, my mother had also been brave enough to raise another topic with the headmaster – the annual poetry recital competition. She had been very aware ... No, I admit I made her very aware of my acute anxiety as each annual poetry competition loomed closer.

The headmaster agreed to try a scheme that was quite successful and saved me from utter humiliation in my last year. When I stood up to take my turn, he would, sitting at the back of the audience so they could not see him, mouth the poem in sync with me. This worked well, allowing me to produce a reasonably fluent recital. That year it was *The River's Tale*. What is more, the headmaster was very pleased to have been able to help. Just a pity it came so late in my time at his school.

During school holidays, my mother and I would visit sundry speech therapists. The long and worrying road through a seemingly endless series of speech therapists has become somewhat blurred in my mind. This is probably because I tended to try and ignore my stammer – hoping I could just carry on. For as soon as it became an acknowledged problem, it seemed to get worse and cause greater interference in my life. I recall attending various interviews and examinations – none of them very pleasant or easy experiences for me. It seemed to me that most doctors and speech therapists had one aim in view: they wanted to get me to relax and so breathe more slowly. Obviously I was too uptight and fraught to speak fluently and I did tend to take a sudden intake of breath whenever I got stuck on a word. It was at one of these relax-and-breathe sessions, when I was about nine years old, that I had my first erotic – or at least sort of erotic – experience.

I can see the room now. It was high ceilinged with huge great windows – perhaps an old school or even a grand if now very former, Georgian drawing room. It was very light, sunlit and airy. The floor was wooden – worn and polished boards, not parquet blocks. There were lots of black cushions and bolsters around. I was lying on the floor under strict and persistent orders to relax. If I was relaxed, I would breathe more slowly and easily and then – magically – not stammer. Exasperated at failing to make me to relax, this thirty-ish and bouncy female therapist lay down beside me on the floor. I raised my head a bit and looked down to see her long bare legs lying beside mine – it must have been summertime:

> 'Now, imagine your arms and legs are like ripe plums hanging heavily off their trees – or bunches of juicy blackcurrants weighing down their branches – or even a bunch of grapes – drooping and loose, just hanging there – heavy and oh so relaxed.'

Bunches of grapes? It seemed only a couple of years earlier I had seen my first bunch of bananas.

My response to this was to freeze. She picked up one of my arms and then let it go. It did not drop down like a heavy bunch of blackcurrants (I had at least had practise picking blackcurrants) or plums (I knew a lot about stewed plums – unacceptably sour due to sugar rationing). My arm stayed up in the air – straight and rigid. Far from being relaxed, I was very tense. She sighed and took my hand and plonked it firmly on one of her breasts: 'There – that's what being relaxed feels like.' And she kneaded her breast with my hand. I don't think that made me relax. Though this sort of therapy certainly felt different – interesting – rather exciting. But in all my subsequent speech therapy outings it never happened again. The upsides of stammering were few and far between.

With relaxation came – or rather should have come – controlled breathing. This was something I was supposed to practise on my own and frequently. However, it just did not work for me. I was convinced that breathing just happened. The rate of intake of air depended, I was certain, on the amount of energy you were using. So running up hill meant deeper breaths and so on. Controlling my breathing was not really my job. So I thought.

I do recall one occasion when I was forced to admit that it might be helpful to my stammering speech if I could bring myself to face this breathing thing. I was staying with my father's sister, Aunt Nell, on her farm in Warwickshire. It had been a long and tiring day riding the sled behind the baler and then I had made some mistake with the calves' food. I was in a tizz and Aunt Nell suggested I should have a long and hot pre-bedtime bath. Midway through this, Aunt Nell knocked and came into the bathroom. As any thirteen-year-old boy with a low embarrassment threshold might do, I rolled over onto my stomach. As the bathwater cooled and the summer light faded, we had a long conversation. She told me more about my father's love of horses than I had ever heard before. I told Aunt Nell about my desire to have a pony and how my friend Libby had helped me learn about horses and riding. She told me stories of the time before the war when she drove horse boxes for a racing trainer.

Eventually, I began to shiver in the tepid water and Aunt Nell made to leave: 'There you are you see – you don't always need to stammer. Lying on your front must have helped your breathing and you've not stammered once in the past fifteen minutes. It's all about breathing – I used to say that to your father too.' 'Right,' I said, 'I'll remember that – and what you told Daddy. Thank you.' 'Just think how pleased he'd be if you got over your stammer – I would be too.' And she gave her chummy Aunt Nell laugh.

I was not taking well to the various speech therapists – whether they concentrated on relaxation or breathing. It seems I was simply not a determined enough person when it came to following speech therapists' guidance and exhortations to 'please keep practising this at home'. One trying-to-be-helpful adult suggested I had probably reached a double bind stage: my stammer was a terrible nuisance and stopped me talking to all sorts of people, but it had also become a defence. Because of the stammer I did not need to try making conversation – or even, at school, to answer in class. Certainly, as I grew into long trousers, a theory that said my stammer was a necessary defence against a world my stammer would not allow me to join, withered to irrelevance as teenage beckoned. Especially when it came to talking with girls.

It may have been the Spring after my holiday with Aunt Nell that my mother ran out of local social service/medical type speech therapists and spotted an advertisement. A man with a load of letters after his name was promising to help with 'speech impediments and similar problems in young and old'. The brief text explained he had developed a new theory and technique after years spent teaching young female opera singers how to make the most of their vocal chords.

Yes, he would help me. I think the fee was £150 for four morning sessions – a lot of money in those days. He lived miles away, but luckily close to some family friends I had never knowingly met and whose family structure was a mystery to me. I was sent off to stay with them and make my way on the four appointed mornings by bus to his house. I should digress here to say that apart from shopkeepers (whom we shall meet soon), bus conductors were my least favourite people. To use a bus I almost always had to ask the conductor for a ticket to a destination with a name I could not complete fluently in public. They were busy, it was noisy and it was always harder to state a destination a second time after I had already blurted it out in an array of sounds that foxed bus conductors. As for asking to be dropped off at a particular road, I could easily have stayed silent and ended up at the terminus. Bus conductors were not the most sympathetic people I came across.

Having to make small talk with a family I did not know and having to talk to bus conductors, left me in a bit of a state. So it was not really very surprising that the four sessions left no impression on my stammer whatsoever. The man's theory should have raised immediate suspicions. He believed impediments to speech or underwhelming use of a singing voice were due to a deformation of the rear of the tongue – a depression where there should be none. I was close to panic: how was he going to reshape the back of my tongue without some kitchen surgery? 'Relax,' he said. Oh no! Not more relaxation. 'Relax – it's a matter of exercising the tongue so it knows how to behave when you speak.' He produced a piece of clear plastic or Perspex shaped rather like an open spanner with a spatula-like handle. This was his unique selling point. It was used to depress the outside parts of the tongue so the depression in the middle of the tongue vanished. Voila! Simple stuff? Certainly simplistic stuff.

However, the game was somewhat given away when, between bouts of exercising with the see-through-spanner-thing, we did lots and lots of slow reading. It was not, after all, just about the tongue – it was about slowing down one's speech, even about relaxing it! The slow reading was recorded onto a wire audio recorder and then played back to hear where I had 'gone wrong'. I did learn one thing from those front-room sessions in a gloomy semi in a leafy suburb: I simply loathe hearing my speech played back to me. This new recording technology may have worked a treat on impressionable young opera singers who probably thought their voices were top notch before their ambitious mothers sent them to the 'tongue doctor'. His ritual and optimistic gabbling simply reduced me to tears. On the last morning, he said it might be a good idea if I got back to my digs in time for lunch. We said goodbye. So I was leaving early, none too gently ejected from the front room, bearing the piece of plastic – or Perspex – and wondering how I was going to explain this costly failure to my mother.

It is very difficult, looking back nearly seventy years, to judge how seriously I took my stammer at various stages of my childhood. One precise measure comes from my reaction to King George VI's stammer – in particular, of course, to his Christmas messages on the wireless. For many years we spent Christmas with my maternal grandmother and her other daughter, my 'Favourite Aunt', Nicie. Christmas Day was church, then a late full-trappings lunch, quick clearance and washing up, followed the King's address. At which point I took myself as far from the wireless as Granny's sitting room allowed – usually hiding behind the sofa so I could block my ears and not be told I was being rude to the King. I simply could not bear to hear the King's attempts to get through his address. I felt embarrassed for him, I felt for him, and I was cross that someone had made him struggle through his words in such a public way. The three older women in my life – mother, aunt and grandmother – all said how brave he was and how good the words were that he spoke. I was just silent. And, I think, quite shocked. I found it almost cruel that he was made to deliver this public message. That reaction must have been at or before Christmas 1951 – the last Christmas before the King died. So I can say with some accuracy that this knowing reaction, which reflected the self-awareness I had at the time about my own stammer, came when I was between seven and nine.

Shopping was a major hurdle for me – and one I sometimes flunked. My most frequent shopping chore was to walk to the local grocer for bread and milk. There were two characters in the grocery shop who have left lasting images with me. One was the owner – or perhaps joint owner with her husband. Mrs Karn was roundabout, calm, business-like, but kind. She often looked as though grocery problems weighed very heavily on her rounded shoulders. The other was a stick thin, brittle looking lady with peroxided hair and a faux-plummy enunciation. She did not take kindly to my stammered requests. She seemed to be counting the wasted seconds. Belying her size, she had a deep smoker's voice: 'Hurry up. Do hurry up.' This made me embarrassed as the queue formed behind me, and so those 'wasted seconds' mounted up. I remember at least one occasion when there was stalemate. She would not take the time to unravel my request – so I was reduced to leaning right over the counter and pointing at the jar or packet of whatever it was that had been added to the usual milk and bread shopping list. This was not approved of at all. I was barked at very loudly and as I pushed back to stand on the floor, I knocked something off the counter. What it was has been wiped from my memory. But I am pretty sure it was not serious enough to involve broken glass or eggshells.

I will now admit that on occasion, when the shopping list included something I knew I would not be able to ask for in public, I would come home and say the shop had run out of it. The introduction of self-help supermarkets – even village-sized ones – came just in time. I soon switched my allegiance to the grocer beside the village green who had installed select-it-yourself shelves and a checkout with a man who did not want to ask after my mother or the weather or if I knew whether the blackberries were ripe enough to pick. His name was Mr Challis. Several people in the village railed against this new 'supermarket' – as though content that asking for items the assistant or grocer had to go and fetch, kept them securely in a master-servant relationship. To me, Mr Challis was a help-yourself hero.

While we are shopping, I should mention my fear of hairdressers. The nearest hairdresser to home was in the town five miles away. It was very much a gentlemen's parlour. It sold fishing tackle. Its walls were covered with glass cases of stuffed fish caught in the nearby River Wey – larger than anything my brother or I ever caught in its tangled waters. It had a calm and very quiet feel to it – almost like being in church save for the gentle clipping clatter of scissors and some buzzing of electric clippers. There was also a warning murmur of chat. You waited your turn on green leather seats opposite the row of complicated chairs and deep basins. You could see each customer reflected in the mirror. I think you were supposed to mind your ps and qs and not stare at the mirrors but read, mark and learn from old copies of *Country Life* and *The Field*.

Waiting my turn was torture. I knew when I got into the chair that my barber would try and start an earnest conversation. That was his intention. He soon discovered that my responses were limited to sounds rather than words. The expectation that my haircut would be interrupted with stammering, led without fail to worse stammering. I knew that sometimes when I stammered badly the effort made my head move in small jerks. I was terrified that if I got involved on a long sentence or two, it could involve a jerk or two too far and I might then lose part of an ear or get nicked in my neck. I came to hate having my hair cut so much that once we were married, Alison used to cut what was left of it. She became an expert at cutting my hair. Only after I retired did I find someone who did not expect me to talk, but to whom I could talk quite easily and often fluently – she never pushed for an answer to her questions and never finished a word for me. She is called Ingrid.

Although I was burdened with poor teeth – the wartime lack of natural calcium was blamed – I did not really mind the indignities of the juddering drill, the awful coming round after gas and the inevitable Novocain needles. It all meant, as one's mouth filled with cotton wool and metal instruments, you did not have to talk to the dentist. The odd throaty grunt was quite enough. It was not quite the same when I first had to wear glasses. The temptation not to say a difficult letter on the optician's chart could have landed me with stronger glasses and damaged eyes. I compromised with 'I think its D' or M or ...

From about the age of nine or ten, during those school holidays on Aunt Nell's farm, I was treated to a meal at a posh restaurant near Stratford-upon-Avon. In the summer holidays such a treat usually marked another field successfully harvested. At home we only ate out with Granny at the local pub's lunchtime restaurant – and fierce Granny ordered for us all. It was on these occasions with Aunt Nell that I discovered the pitfalls of ordering from a menu.

The waiter was usually tall, towering oppressively over me, and often impatient. I was trying hurriedly to balance the dishes I could name fluently against those I might enjoy. Then I heard the 'And young sir?' and I rushed into choosing the ham salad. 'Ham' was easy for me to say, which was a good thing as we lived in Ham Lane. After I had made the same choice at three of those treats, my assumed penchant for 'ham salad' became a family joke. Later on, ordering in pubs and restaurant was another of the hurdles I would face – right up to the present. I have certainly missed numerous delicious dishes because I shied away from their tripwire sounds. Or one can resort to pointing at the selected dish on the menu. This may be allowable in a country whose language, if you attempt it, is likely to leave the waiter baffled and cross. I have pointed to more choices on British, Irish and American menus than I care to remember. That sort of menu pointing never leaves me feeling good.

Did my stammer stifle my social life up to and including my teenage years? Was I really as shy as I recall? On 14 October 1944 my father had written to my mother: 'I like A.J. only playing amongst friends and not before strangers!' Hmm. It was only a handful of years later that I saw myself as being like 'the cat that walked by himself' – a solitary child. My father had been a Kipling aficionado and taking over his duties, my mother read the *Just So Stories* to me as I refused to lie down and go to sleep – perhaps scared of the dreams that lay ahead. I particularly liked the black and white illustrations in my father's edition of Kipling's tales: especially the rear view of the cat as he starts his lonely way along an avenue of winter trees. It certainly fixed in my mind the rather solitary nature of my life. Kipling's style was as close as we got in our home to 'magical': *'Hear and attend and listen; for this befell and behappened and became and was, O my Best Beloved, when the Tame animals were wild.'* I can still feel the excitement in those strange words. He would have made a great propagandist ... perhaps he was one.

As I grew older it was hard getting to know people when I was loath to launch into a proper conversation with them. Some people of my own age were fine and just ignored the stammer. Some I felt so at ease with that my stammer simply faded. Some froze when I started to talk – and that was the end of that. But it probably says as much about my personality as about my stammer (though I continue to believe they were closely interlinked) that with many people I just did not try. It was too much effort and I was too likely to fail.

A school holiday visit to a Christian 'camp' gives one example of my stammer's 'glass ceiling'. I was dispatched there one summer as it offered (apparently) a sure-fire 'get him out of himself' cure. Was I really that bad? It was held in an empty school in Norfolk – and we sailed on the Broads. Each boy took a turn at the tiller. When it was my turn, I got absolutely stuck on with the 'Ready about – lee ho' and we hit the bank with a terrible thud. A grown-up was almost catapulted into the rather murky water. Other boys giggled and blushed. I went white. So white I was asked if I was about to faint. Anyway, that successfully excised 'World Champion Sailor' from my list of possible future achievements.

The stammer also made getting to know girls much more difficult. Of course it did. The girl next door was okay – I could wave to her over the garden fence and call for her to come over for a chat and a game of draughts or to hunt for caterpillars – and then one of our walks with no hand holding. Then the lovely Diana went to a grammar school and found her own friends.

My first long-term love/crush lived a fifteen-minute walk from home – Libby. She had a lovely mother and an ever-smiling father. She was obsessed with horses. In fact, she taught me a great deal about horses and riding. My mother, in better times a respected rider herself, told me Libby had an excellent seat and the straightest of backs. She added that Libby did not smile very much. I knew differently, she smiled a lot when we were together. She used to let me cycle alongside as she exercised her horse on the nearby common. She was, however, instrumental in my first fall off a horse – not a pony, a fully 16.2 hands worth of horse. She had given me a leg up and said I knew enough to try a small jump. I was to take her horse (I wish I could remember its name), over a fallen tree – quite a hefty trunk. She stood the other side encouraging her horse to make the jump. Then, suddenly, she spotted a piece of broken glass on the landing zone. 'Oh no!' She bent to pick it up. Her sudden movement startled the horse which reared back from the log, sending me slithering to the ground, luckily missing the tree trunk. To my delight she just smiled: 'Sorry, my fault but perhaps a little bit firmer with the knees.'

This friendship came at a cost. I would spend hours walking on past her house, turning round, coming back again, checking the rear drive to see whether she was there grooming her horse: all the time trying to pluck up courage to ring the front doorbell. Often, when I finally got to ring the bell, I would be turned beetroot red by her lovely mother calling loudly: 'Libby, where are you? Your boyfriend's here'. At least she never added 'Again!' She was much too good a person for that. Of course what I was supposed to do, what every other boy I knew did, was to make a telephone call to a girl before setting out – even if you got through to a parent: 'Please can I come and see Libby? ... Well, yes, a cup of tea would be really nice. Thank you ... I'll be with you very soon ... Yes, I can help cleaning tack ... No I won't mind at all ... love to do it.'

To be with Libby, I would have agreed to clean the drains. But telephoning ahead to invite myself was out of the question. We shall, I fear, return to this case of extreme phone phobia.

'Libby' was fairly difficult for me to say smoothly – another tight 'i' following a fairly hard 'l'. The Jane, the Sarah and the Anne (all easy sounds for me) lived too far away for me to simply walk over, turning up on the off chance. They would need a phone call and that risked stammering away to a parent. There was always a risk in making a telephone call, even a risk in answering the telephone when my mother was out. One of the first lessons my stammer taught me once I began to need to make telephone calls, was that it is impossible to tell whether that noise coming from other end of the line is embarrassed laughter, shocked laughter or mocking laughter.

There was one thing closely connected to my stammer about which I can be absolutely certain. My move to 'big school' was predicated on what sort of institution would allow my stammer and I to survive in one piece. That was what my understanding mother told me about choosing my next school.

3.

THE NOT QUITE SO BIG
SCHOOL

The end of my first boarding school was in sight and the dreaded Common Entrance exam was approaching (how I hate exams – I got so worked up about the Eleven Plus they would not let me take it). The leap that would take me to my next school was concerning my mother. She had seen me and my stammer struggle through one boarding school and feared what might happen to me as I stammered my way through a large, rough and tumble senior school.

Despite putting the war and the killing of her husband behind her, my mother revered his story and achievements. And despite holding to such resolute silence about his death and their life together, she wore her regimental brooch with pride. She saw Andrew through Haileybury & Imperial Service College, and I am certain I was on course to follow him there. At that time Haileybury had about 650 boys. Apart from the impact of my stammer on the decision, there was the little matter of how to pay the fees. Not easy on a war widow's pension. I do know that in 1945 my mother 'could just about manage' with Andrew's reduced fees at the junior school. Before I went to the same school, the headmaster had written to my mother:

'This is to assure you that of course we want Anthony to come here & that I am absolutely prepared to take him at the same reduced fees that any of these other schools are offering, or at any fees which would help you educate him here ... Please do not worry about this matter any more.'

I am certain the headmaster reduced my fees at that school. Much later my mother told me that the Haileybury memorial fund paid a significant proportion of my fees at my second, 'not so big', boarding school. This was amazingly generous. I wish I had been able to say thank you – especially for the burden this lifted from my mother.

My new school was in Gloucestershire. It had about 320 boys, nearly all of them boarders. Among them was the elder son of our best friends in the village – who would, I was assured, look after me. It had been founded in 1886 as a school for the sons of Church of England clergy, but had long since taken sons of any-old-body. It had a comprehensive style mixture of students – from the blindingly brilliant to the 'please will you take my boy he's not learnt anything yet'. They included some eccentrics – for instance the farmer's son who kept a .410 shotgun under his dormitory bed. At first light in summertime, he went out onto the nearby network of railway embankments to shoot rabbits. No one quite knew if they ended up in the school's lunchtime stews or whether he sold them to a local butcher – perhaps he had a supply contract.

I started there in September 1955. Term after term the train journeys to school were hell and the arrival grim. The only pluses were my house master and his wife – Arnold and Elaine. Their support and friendship lasted throughout my five years there. Arnold Parker was also my utterly brilliant English teacher. Elaine was in her late twenties – they had two children. I believe that during the first year at this school I went once a week to see a speech therapist at her private house. Then in my second year I went to a speech therapy clinic at the local hospital. I know this for certain because from January to June 1956 I kept a kind of diary. This charts my weekly visits to the hospital clinic: 'Go to hospital at 5.30 as normal, but when we got there we found that Miss Braithwaite is ill!' I have no recollection at all as to who 'we' were (perhaps Arnold took me there by car) or what Miss Braithwaite was like or what approach she took to speech therapy. However, I don't think I had too much faith in the effectiveness of those clinic visits. By 23 May my skeletal diary records: 'Decided to cut the speech therapy out, so don't go.'

Re-reading this diary for the first time in sixty-five years has been a terrible shock. I have always realised I was not very mature when I got to this school – a continuing 'late developer'. Having very poor handwriting was one thing, having terrible spelling was just awful. 'Waist' for 'waste, 'supper' frequently with one p, 'speach' instead of 'speech'. Yet my vocabulary was pretty good. I did take care in this diary to underline in red every mention of Libby – notably the arrival of her letters. Yet the incomplete bundle of termly school reports show that I was doing well in class. One term I even came top of the class, with the headmaster adding: 'Very good – developing well.' Perhaps the standards at the school were lower than my mother had been promised.

These reports make little reference to my stammer. In the report for Lent Term 1956 Arnold did write: 'His stammer seems less than it was.' And at the end of the summer term that year: 'His stammer improves and his self confidence grows.' But by the end of the following Lent term things were slipping backwards: 'Perhaps he is a touch more self-conscious than he was and his stammer is a bit variable.' In my second year in the sixth form, I became a house prefect and at the end of that term Arnold reported: 'He has been most successful as a house prefect despite his handicap ...' (I would blush to continue that sentence).

Now that is the first time I have ever seen my stammer referred to as a 'handicap'. That stops me in my tracks for I do not remember my stammer registering then at the 'handicap' level. There were plenty of blips and problems. French oral was a continual problem and my O Level oral exam was only saved from total disaster by a charming and very young female examiner who decided to make it into a chat led by as many French words and phrases as I could muster. I would have willingly gone back into that examination room for another round.

From time to time I would ask if Arnold could please suggest to one or other of his staffroom colleagues that they should give me more of a chance to answer in class. That did not always work out as I hoped: I can see the room now with the physics master perched on one of the laboratory work benches. It was about movement, speed and forces: 'What's it called when forces make an object gather speed?' He pointed a finger at me and I began to say the word: 'A-a-a-c-c ...' 'Well,' he interrupted, 'I know Millett knows the word. Anyone else?' Silence. Were they embarrassed for me? Probably not. Probably merely confused or thinking about tomorrow's hockey matches or the headmaster's secretary. So rather than giving me a second go, he continued: 'The word is, of course, acceleration.' Did that upset me? Funnily enough at the time 'No' – after all, the teacher knew I knew the right answer and he was being, in his terms, helpful and friendly. However, as with similar episodes, it did set me thinking. Would it always be like this? Would I ever be able to hold down a job? Would I ever find a serious, grown-up girlfriend who understood? And so, round and round in my head – enough to wilt my concentration on physics and its forces.

In one of the termly reports, the headmaster referred to my 'difficult years of adolescence'. At least for the first three years I was not a very happy schoolboy. Everything seemed to be a struggle – largely due to the stammer. By turns, I was on the dejected side of miserable. This reached a peak in my third year when I was summoned from my bed soon after lights out. In the senior common room the desks and chairs were back against the walls and a cross within a circle chalked on the wood block floor. I was told to take off my dressing gown, stand on the chalk mark and bend over. While in that position I was lectured by the head of house: 'We don't like your attitude. How are you going to change it?' I had no idea and said so. I may then have said I was worried about my O Level exams. Whatever. He slapped a very large gym shoe on the palm of his hand and sighed: 'OK – back to the dormitory. And shape up.' Shape up? He must have been reading trashy American thrillers. There was, of course, no mention of my stammer, but I am certain it was the root cause of my supposedly problematic 'attitude'. At least I was none the worse for the evening's interruption. In my fourth year, entering the sixth form, I cheered up no end.

During the 1960 Easter holidays, while I was busy revising for the A Level exams, my mother and I reached a decision about my future – and for my part it hinged on my stammer. I could go back to school for a third year in the sixth form and take university entrance exams. Or I could leave school and spend part of the following academic year with a firm of tutors in London. It seemed to me there was a single deciding factor: going back to school meant becoming a school prefect and that involved public speaking – saying grace before meals, making announcements and readings during chapel services. I was caught in what was for me a familiar dilemma. I could agree to be a school prefect and struggle on regardless, or they could make me a special case so I would not have to do the public speaking. Neither seemed palatable enough to my eighteen-year-old self – so I plumped for the tutor in London.

This was probably a mistake. In retrospect most probably a fairly minor mistake. It certainly annoyed the headmaster. I suspect that at the start of the summer term I took a letter to him from my mother saying I would be leaving at the end of that term. On 12 May 1960 he replied to my mother:

'I am not really sure it is best for Anthony to leave as I imagine he might well have been a School Prefect next year. He has come on a lot this last 12 months and at last seems to be getting rid of the worst features of his stammer, and what a charming person he is too. Thank you very much for sending him to us ...'

However, when he came to write my final school report, he was to say the least pretty darn cross:

> 'I am very sorry to lose him and disappointed that, after bringing him through the difficult years of adolescence, and after building up his confidence, we are not having the return from his year of office & authority that this good boy would have given us. I hope for his sake that he will get the necessary experience at his tutor's. We shall follow his career with interest and, I hope, pride.'

Wow. I wish I'd known how my mother reacted to that broadside.

During those five years I also had to negotiate the anxiety surrounding my mother's deteriorating health. In 1956, after a number of worrying new symptoms appeared, she went into St Thomas' Hospital for tests. This must have been about 30 October–1 November – the dates of the rowdy Parliamentary debates over the Suez Crisis – or fiasco. She told me that lying in a hospital bed just across the River Thames from the Houses of Parliament, she wanted to open a window and scream at them for behaving like idiots and plead with them to stop the invasion. She was, after all, a card carrying and active member of the United Nations Association.

The lumbar puncture confirmed her worst fears – she had multiple sclerosis (MS). (Later it became fairly certain that her presumed polio before the war had in fact been a first bout of MS, after which she had gone into a long remission, as can happen with that cruel disease.) The stress of knowing that she was still living on her own and crawling up stairs to bed every night was grim. Arnold and Elaine gave me frequent support and advice.

Frankly, it was a huge relief when my grandmother died in 1957 and my mother and her sister bought a house in the village together. Eventually, as the MS took greater hold, my 'favourite aunt' Nice (sometimes spelt Nicie and always pronounced Nee-see) became her great support and carer.

For those fifteen terms in Gloucestershire I had kept myself to myself – as far as I could. This was, of course, one way to avoid the consequences of the stammer. I am not sure whether I was actively involved in the school's Boycott Committee – taking action against South Africa's apartheid regime. But I certainly joined the plan to carry a symbolic coffin from the school to Trafalgar Square – walking all the way. We thought this might get some headlines. The plan was cancelled at the last minute on 'advice' from a parent of one of the participants. Perhaps that should read 'wise advice'. Even in those distant days, the A40 was not a footpath! In March 1960, my reaction to the Sharpeville Massacre was such that I overcame my stammer sufficiently to collect protest signatures in Cheltenham – on The Promenade no less. It was then not a town awash with people overflowing with liberal empathy. However, I did persuade an on duty police constable to sign. Perhaps he took pity on my stammer.

Understandably, school debates were out of bounds to me. And I was never involved in dramatic productions – on or off the stage. We were close enough to Stratford-upon-Avon to have regular 'trips' to classic Shakespeare: Paul Robeson as *Othello* (1959), Michael Redgrave in *Much Ado* (1958) and Vanessa Redgrave and Diana Rigg in walk-on parts – *All's Well That Ends Well* (1959). These visits gave me a real taste for the excitement of theatre. I had caught the theatre bug. Considering my speech problems, this was unwise – it certainly led to a minor, future disaster.

Regrets? Yes – many. But especially that I never formed friendships there that I could subsequently maintain. I blame a mix of causes. Mainly, undoubtedly, the stammer, which made me wary of friends' parents. There was also the home situation. It was not until university that I invited friends to our new home. It was during those school years that I began to resent the fact that my stammer made me so different and prevented me from talking easily to most adults and making friends among my peers. One episode during the Christmas holidays still makes me cross with myself. Being very short of money, I begged, via a friend of my mother, a place on a local farmer's team of beaters for his annual shoot. I remember trying to open conversations with some of the team as we waited for the next drive. But the stammer won the day so decisively that when the shoot was over I did not dare go back to the keeper's cottage to collect my £5. Instead I went home – very cross.

That was all about not being brave enough to initiate conversations – on the grounds that I might stammer so much it would turn into a defeat. It became a major hurdle when it came to meeting girls. One of my mother's favourite expressions fitted me well: I was nearly always 'backward at coming forward'. I remember one cloudy summer's day, soon after I had passed my driving test, I drove a girl down to the seaside for a swim and a picnic. She was very mature and very attractive with an open face, very dark eyes, a gentle smile, a scatter of freckles and long legs. We had a good if somewhat chilly day beside the sea at West Wittering. After our second swim in rather a rough sea, as we were drying ourselves off, I was so taken by the way she looked with sea water dripping onto her shoulders, I asked Angela if she would mind if I kissed her. Certainly a challenging request for any young man, but for me it came with an added risk: 'kiss' and its hard 'k' followed by the quiet 'i' was a trigger word for my stammer. It was not a word I used very often, but this time, praise be, I got it out. To my utter surprise Angela said: 'Course I won't mind.' So I did. 'That was nice.' I think I was so shocked that we had a rather silent drive home. I did not know what I should try to say next. I don't mention this lightly. That I remember it so clearly shows how important it was for me to be able to talk naturally to people – male and female. Who had said, 'That was nice'? She had. Something to smile about.

On the other hand, I do remember with great pleasure the weeks after the A Level exams. I and fellow sixth formers in my house were at last treated as grown-ups. We had suppers with Arnold and Elaine. We went into town for Chinese meals. And I was taken by Arnold and David (the Head of Music who – thankfully – had introduced me to the delights of classical music) to see a College play at Oxford. I don't remember anything about the play, but I do clearly remember holding my own in a lengthy argument about careers. David thought it was entirely improper for me to go to university without knowing how I was going to earn a living. With Arnold's support, I argued that university was all about finding that out. I suspect the argument arose from my telling them as we drove to Oxford, that I had rejected the advice that I should become a solicitor.

My mother had paid good money for me to see a man from the Schools' Career Advisory Service. I had a wishy-washy interview with this Advisor. He tried very hard not to mention my stammer.

Eventually after a long silence while he consulted my school file, he told me I should become a solicitor. I was so surprised that I spluttered out a challenge. I had seen films or television programmes where solicitors appeared in court not just in silent support of clients, but to speak on their behalf. 'How,' I asked him, 'could I do that?' 'You'll grow out of it – I'm sure'. 'What if I don't and I'm stuck being a solicitor? I will have to be a solicitor who never appears in court – and that is no good to me at all'. At which point he closed the file and said he would be writing to my mother. I was dismissed.

So to London and the tutor.

4.

A GAP YEAR –
NO PASSPORT NEEDED

My post-school, London year was divided into two parts. The first was attending the tutor to sharpen up my Eng Lit and get me 'exam ready'. I lived as a paying guest at the Holland Park home of a literary lioness from a bygone era and sat two Oxford scholarship exams – unsuccessfully. I spent the second part commuting to the City of London working for a Discount House – a City institution whose purpose was somewhat opaque. It was a very educational if, by current standards, a somewhat atypical 'gap year'. Once again, with my first day at the tutors looming, I faced all the usual worries – speaking in public and so on. I must have mentioned this to my mother. The result was one of the worst experiences of my stammering life.

My mother had mentioned my state of stress to a friend of hers. She, in turn, mentioned that her RAF husband had recently retired and was working for the British branch of Dale Carnegie – the American company that publishes self-help books like its founder's *How to Win* [sic] *Friends and Influence People* and *The Art of Public Speaking*. They also ran leadership courses for business people – and were launching courses for young people starting out on life. This ex-RAF man thought one of their courses would solve all my problems. We met briefly at his house. I was speedily persuaded (against, I promise, my better judgement) to go to London and attend a Dale Carnegie open evening at a hotel in Victoria. It was a bit of a blur, but the evening went something like this:

The room was decorated with bunting, balloons and Dale Carnegie book covers and slogans. It was full of people who seemed to me to be young freeloaders hoping the drinks being served might have a smidgen of alcohol in them. I got talking to a very tall – probably 'willowy' – Australian student who told me she was on an exchange and was sharing a bedsit in Earl's Court. Then, perhaps not getting too much sense out of me, she said she had spent the day preparing her two minute-long speech about the future. What? Surely not. No one had warned me about that. I was wondering whether I had better escape right away, when an ex-RAF hand clutched my shoulder: 'Anthony!' (Yes – we all had rather large name tags pinned to our clothes.) 'So glad you could make it – we're about to start – so I'll catch you later.' Then the ex-RAF man turned to the Australian lass (whose name tag name I have forgotten): 'Hello – er – Maxine [or similar], would you kick off the speeches?' She blushed, added a 'yes please' look, and we were away.

How many times have I sat at a meeting – usually round a large table – and heard the chairperson say: 'Perhaps we should just start by introducing ourselves – just round the table – I'll just start ...'? All those 'justs' as though it's not really worth saying at all. Nothing to see here ... It is an even more daunting, more terrifying experience than that early school reading round aloud the class. You have to say your name, job title, employer (if appropriate) and why you're there. But that evening with the Carnegiens, it was much, much worse – worse by a long and sweaty chalk. After Maxine had told us how she wanted to make the world a better place and have babies, the RAF finger pointed at the next victim. And so on, till it was aimed at me and I moved in a state of panic to the microphone.

I have no idea at all what I tried to talk about – bird life? The theatre? Who knows? I have wiped it from my memory. Perhaps with a captive audience I should have had a go at the evils of Apartheid. I can only say that it was an absolute and unmitigated disaster. I don't think I produced many whole words. I certainly produced quite a lot of tittering from the young crowd in front of me. No one came up to help me, let alone to rescue me, or to stop me. And well before my time was up I walked away, collected my coat and left. I am very seldom angry. But this seriously humiliating experience made me very angry indeed. Going home on the train, I tried to work out how this speech therapy by ordeal was supposed to work. This was like a sink or swim trial that in the Middle Ages passed for jurisprudence. To make it so much worse, the aftermath was not at all pretty. Recriminations flew around for several days. My mother had thought it might help – and was distressed. The ex-RAF man was distressed at my distress and, via his distressed wife, sent an apology. Not a good start to my exciting gap year.

The idea of going to a tutor had been welcome and would, I had frequently reassured myself, be a positive change from the restrictions of school. Then, as the idea turned into fast approaching reality, I found myself frozen with fear as to what I would have to do. Would we be in large classes? Would I be expected to read out essays or discuss issues in front of a whole class of all-but-adult students? As it turned out it was so laid-back as to be ridiculous. We did have the occasional one-to-one – or one-to-two or three – tutorials. It all depended on how many staff turned up that day. These tutorials were generally helpful. Homework was almost solely reading – with a very occasional essay set to a suitably lengthy, laid-back deadline. The only part of this new and strange learning experience that had a strict deadline was paying the monthly invoice.

There were some large class discussions. But I need not have worried. They were dominated by a cocky young fellow from one of the cockier third tier public schools. He was going, he assured anyone within earshot, to read English at Cambridge. What about the exam and interview, we asked? Phoo-ee, he just knew he was going to Downing College. Some bright spark teacher at his school had introduced him to FR Leavis and he took to this controversial critic and academic with all the fervour of a newly converted religious zealot. Every time tutors tried to get us to discuss a book or topic, we faced a one-man diatribe on what Leavis would make of it and why it had to be seen through 'the Leavis prism'. At least it meant that I was not called on very often to reveal my stammer, let alone my comparative ignorance of what he delighted in calling 'the Leavis oeuvre'.

Another challenge during those months came with my landlady, Miss Eva Ducat. She was 82 and in her detached house in Holland Park was looked after by a German lady called 'the help', who lived in the basement, cleaned, shopped and cooked. The 'help' had an engaging small child. Eva was of an earlier era, but was remarkably broad-minded. She had known a great list of pre-war literary figures – including DH Lawrence who she said, with a quick flick of her eyes, was a very handsome man. While I was perched in her house, I and my fellow student lodger could join her for dinner one or twice a week. This was sometimes informal and we would help ourselves to hot dishes kept warm over little paraffin burners. But some evenings she had guests – important guests – and we were served at table.

I remember a terribly fraught dinner in the presence of a major figure from the publishing world – the Chairman of Faber and Faber no less. He was the sort of person with whom most teenagers with fluent speech would find it hard to hold a decent, intelligent conversation. I was on the back foot. This meal was, however, enlivened by her asking me to remind her where her other paying guest (studying at the Royal Veterinary College) hailed from. 'B ... I think it's B..B..asingstoke'. 'Oh,' said Eva, laughing off my stammered reply, 'No gentleman ever came from Basingstoke.' She roared with laughter. Whereupon the VIP guest told her off: 'No. No. It's all changed since the war, y'know. Basingstoke's thriving.' I have lately discovered that the delightful Eva was born in Andover – just up the road from Basingstoke.

During these months I made two excursions to Oxford in search of a scholarship at best or entrance at any rate, and one to Nottingham in search of a place. It was difficult to stay the night at two Oxford Colleges – Worcester and Exeter – and not to make a serious investigation into the town's pubs before sitting an exam and the dreaded interview. At Exeter I made a pact with a chap called George from Bolton School to have no more than one pint. The Exeter paper and interview are however a complete blank, put out of mind and memory by the gruesome Worcester College experience. I had been reading up and writing an essay for the tutors on Jonathan Swift's *Gulliver's Travels*. I realised it was a book that is as complex as it is simple – good for a children's tale, but perhaps best for deep academic theorising. I had found a theory about Swift's intentions and targets that seemed perfect for a learned disquisition at my interview. It came from an American academic and was thick with footnotes. And I knew it backwards. At the interview I managed to turn an answer to Swift – perhaps he was my favourite eighteenth-century author.

The Worcester College Fellow interviewing me was young. I thought he was about the same age as I was. Why was he interviewing me? He must have only just started teaching? I now discover he was the grand old age of twenty-seven. He introduced himself as Christopher. That was as matey as we got. No sooner had I started to explain Swift's intentions and he was onto me, tearing apart every statement I made. I became flustered and began to stammer rather badly. Almost as if in embarrassed retaliation, he interrupted me every time I stammered, leaving me floundering. So this deep and satisfying theory never got past its first footnote. At the end we did not even shake hands. Later on – while he was championing Bob Dylan as a poet – he was one reason I gave up reading *The Sunday Times* in which he appeared regularly as a reviewer who never attempted to suffer those he thought to be fools. Oh dear! Oh Oxford!

Nottingham was a different kettle of fish altogether. I had been told to ask for the Portland Building where someone would direct me. I was sent off to the 'Cowsheds' where a Professor was waiting for me. Not just an upstart Fellow, a real capital 'P' Professor. But 'Cowsheds'? Sure enough, in an office in the English Department's temporary building or 'Cowshed' was the Prof – Vivian de Sola Pinto. Just in case I should meet him on my interview visit, I had asked one of the tutors in London who he was: 'Fought in the First World War, friend of Sassoon, expert on DH Lawrence – especially the poetry – and on Lord Rochester – so better keep off them – and I suppose keep off sex too – you know, Lawrence *and* Rochester.'

When I met him for my admission interview, Professor Vivian de Sola Pinto was on the verge of retirement. It was during my first year at Nottingham University that he hit the headlines with his appearance for the defence in the famous *Lady Chatterley's Lover* trial. He was called as an expert on Lawrence rather than on sex. Old and clubbable as Professor de Sola Pinto looked, when he shook my hand and introduced himself, I was in for a shock. He had a speech impediment too. He repeated the last couple of syllables of the last word in most sentences or phrases he uttered. Together we were left with the middle few words of our conversation *en clair*. And those middle words passed for an interview. Quite a babble. Whether his impediment was the result of his experiences at Gallipoli or with German gas on the Western Front, remains unclear. He does not mention his impediment in his autobiography.

He was, of course, absolutely lovely – calming and giving me time to finish my sentences. I carefully kept off Swift and Rochester (whose connection to sex I knew so little about), but I did venture into Lawrence territory. I told him how I hoped to gain more insight into Lawrence's novels from studying literature in the area of England where he was born and brought up, and being at the university he had attended. The Prof seemed to like that idea:

> 'You will meet our Prof of Economic History, David Chambers. He's the younger brother of Lawrence's first real love, Jessie Chambers. You'll know her as the model for Miriam in *Sons and Lovers*.'

Luckily I did know about Miriam – we had 'done' *Sons and Lovers* at the Tutors. Much later, I certainly remember a student society lecture by Prof Chambers. With his thick Nottinghamshire accent, he told entrancing stories about his young days at Haggs Farm with his sister Jessie and the ever attendant David Lawrence and how they read books together – books by the score. It was amazing to find history so telescoped as to hear his first hand stories from the beginning of the century.

I do recall that my interview with Professor Pinto included a fair amount of bad stammering. But at least he showed no sign whatsoever of being perturbed by my speech. It was only on the train home that I realised Prof de Sola Pinto had, by saying I 'will' meet Jessie's brother, virtually assured me I would have a place in his department. In a few days, a letter duly confirmed my place. I was just sorry I would not have more contact with the wonderful Vivian de Sola Pinto. During my first term at the university I discovered it had been the sport of some English department students to ask their professor questions in such a way as to ensure he ended his reply with the word Coriolanus – repeating, as he often did, the last two syllables. Very droll.

PARTS OF SPEECH 77

Before we come onto the second part of my 'gap year', I should explain how I found being independent and on the loose in the Great Wen. Of course, I loved it. But it had several drawbacks. One of them was the business of getting around London. As I have already made clear, I hated buses. I do not think I took an ad hoc bus journey in London between the day I arrived at Eva Ducat's home to the day I got my first Oyster Card – several decades later. The only exception was for regular journeys to work when I had a weekly season ticket I could flash at bus conductors.

In the early 1960s, underground travel posed me problems that were very similar to those I avoided on buses. Asking for a tube ticket at the ticket office window was a gamble I dreaded taking. But there were in all central London tube stations ticket machines. They were big and blue-grey with a sloping glass top that listed the stations you could buy tickets for. However, they seldom seemed to include the station I wanted. So, needing to use the machines rather than ask at the ticket window, I frequently ended up paying London Transport for a much longer journey and getting off early at the station I needed. I hope they were glad of my generosity. I have read recently that when he was a young boy, Philip Larkin stammered so badly that he would write his destination on a piece of paper and hand it to the ticket office. That was a trick I had not thought of, but trying it would almost certainly have proved too mortifying.

Much, much later on, the introduction of the Oyster Card took away from me, at a stroke, a whole layer of everyday anxiety. No more asking for a ticket, you just put your card on the button-thing and kept an eye out for your stop. You can even add money to it without talking through a hatch to people who seem unwilling to lean forward and ask you to repeat your request slowly. However, technological advances are not always on the stammerer's side. More recent voice-recognition telephone systems often defeat me – leading to a receiver slam down. I usually get stuck on my name or a simple 'Yes' ('If you want to speak to a member of our team say "Yes" now.') Even now I can get so stuck I confuse the software and get 'We didn't quite hear that – please say it again more clearly.' 'No chance!'. Slam.

Jumping a few more years forward, as the digital tide sweeps on, you won't find Alexa – or any of her data-sucking sister clones – in our home. They are simply not sophisticated enough to understand a stammered request. Though that also means they would not be making sense of conversations they're so good at over hearing. The flip side is the arrival of email which has hugely reduced the number of phone calls I have to make. Less amusingly, we increasingly find that our doctor will not see us now, but merely chat with us by phone. For me it may yet prove as difficult as talking to voice recognition robots. So far though I have not had a problem – with a very considerate female doctor.

While I lived at Eva Ducat's home I spent much of my spare time and spare evenings on my own – and I made the most of that often buying the cheapest seats for some of London's best theatrical treats. I saw Judi Dench and John Stride in Franco Zeffirelli's Old Vic *Romeo and Juliet*. And, captivated by Miss Dench, went the following day to hear her and John Stride read poetry at Foyles bookshop. That was a disappointment. Juliet had such a bad cold she could only read a couple of short poems. I was lucky to go twice to *Beyond the Fringe* – once with Libby – and I frequented The Mermaid Theatre's cheap seats. I mention these delights, purely to show that my life at that time was not made totally miserable by my stammer, merely constricted. Seeing so many plays strengthened my interest in the theatre. How I would love to direct a play ... I daydreamed choosing the right play with which to launch my directorial career.

For the second part of my 'gap' year I left Miss Ducat's home and commuted to the City of London from home in Surrey. I was working for one of the smaller Discount Houses – paid work experience. It took me about a week to get my head round what this company actually did. For the most part, it was borrowing the major banks' overnight cash surpluses and lending it to the government in the form of Treasury Bills. The directors were 'bill brokers' and made a small margin on large amounts of money. Paul Ferris in his book *The City* tells of a bill broker who was introduced to the producer of the television hit show *What's My Line?* Could he take part? 'Viewers wouldn't understand what you did. And if they did they wouldn't believe it.' Another view, a Cold War view, I heard was that bill brokers would be first up against the wall if the communists took over the country. I never knew why the banks didn't do the job themselves, and I was not brave enough to ask.

I was working for this small but thrusting Discount House because its chairman lived in the next village to home and one of its directors was the father of two of my local friends. Their tiny offices were just off Lombard Street. It was a friendly office. I would carry cheques round the banks' headquarters, I would fill in record cards, totting up totals, and later collect cheques and carry round more cheques – making sure I got to the right banks and offices before they closed their books. Carrying cheques for

£250,000 and more – at that moment in the twentieth century, six figure sums were significantly eye-popping – made me nervous at first and then made me feel quite important. The great thing about it all was that I was not called on to say very much. By today's digital standards it was all very quaint.

This experience made me quite certain I could never be a commuter. Even with a heavy dose of traditional British froideur, topped up with early morning sleepiness, there was a sense that you should be chatting to people you 'met' in the same compartments of the same trains day after day. That I found very stressful, especially as any chat was so public, so easily overheard. I did warm to the story of the comedian and broadcasting star 'Professor' Jimmy Edwards who at one time commuted to a London office on the same line I used every day. Not wanting to be bothered with chatter and recognition, he buried his head in *The Times'* crossword – scribbling away with his propelling pencil. After a few stations he would smile in victory and turn to the city pages. One day, however, he left his copy on the seat and one of his regular fellow commuters discovered that Edwards had just put any old letters into the crossword squares. The things people do to make sure they don't have to talk to other people.

I had not done any travelling in my 'gap year', but I now had behind me some good experience of the world beyond schools and beyond home. I had become very disenchanted with our home village and with some of the people in it. Our part of Surrey may have been rural and calm, but it was subject to rigid class divisions.

There were several families in the village with which I found it all but impossible to hold a conversation – especially with the fathers. Their 'above the fray' attitude was blatant, but also they were clearly embarrassed by my stammering. So I kept my distance.

From my current, strangely privileged point of retrospection, it is pretty obvious that I had outgrown home. School holidays had become a bit of a burden. I did a lot of very enjoyable reading and a lot of very enjoyable walking. Until I could drive, lack of transport between villages and local towns was a constant hindrance to making and meeting friends. In those days hitch-hiking was the adolescent's key route to freedom. I failed to achieve a single thumbed journey. The fear of having to talk to a stranger on a long journey while trapped in a cab was just too much for me. So passing my driving test and the occasional use of a car was a giant step forward. But I did still spend most of my time at home. Keeping my mother company in the evenings, I watched quite a lot of television. One evening we watched a programme that included demonstrations by a serious looking hypnotist. I did just wonder whether he could help me with my stammer.

So by April 1961 hypnosis had appeared on my stammer to-do list.

5.

'YOU ARE FALLING INTO
A DEEP SLEEP'

We need to pause here and investigate an episode in the life of my stammer for which I have kept no records, but which was very, very important to me. In the absence of my own records, I have been doing a bit of research. Although my mother had tried faith healing for her MS, in our family treatment of any health issue was left strictly to the GP and the NHS. Suddenly pinning my hopes on hypnotism was a bit of a leap into the unknown.

Towards the start of my 'gap year' I decided, with the freedom of university and the perils of employment looming closer, I should try harder to find a definitive cure for my stammer. Somewhere I had picked up on LSD (lysergic acid diethylamide) and its potential use in the treatment of psychiatric conditions – 'LSD-assisted psychotherapy' was a phrase of the moment. Perhaps it was another article in those *Reader's Digest* issues passed on from the lady next door. Or else someone on television mentioned how LSD might be used in the treatment of anxiety. I don't think I believed my stammer was caused by anxiety, but I certainly knew it caused anxiety.

I started to do some gentle digging around. My first port of call was Dr ER Matthews, a GP from Bath who had come to our school to talk about sex – or perhaps to tell us about sex. I actually found his talks rather helpful – in the obvious absence of the more usual and strictly paternal 'It's about time I told you about ...'. In 1959 Dr Matthews published a book – *Sex, Love and Society*. I wrote to Dr Matthews care of his publishers, asking whether he thought LSD could help cure my stammer. To my amazement, he replied – in true private school form:

> 'Dear Millett ... Stammering is a considerable nuisance to the sufferer and treatment of it is notoriously unsatisfactory.'

So far so goodish. In fact, it was a very full and fair letter. He believed a stammer was primarily caused by fear – often of a parent. (Perhaps in my case fear of not having a parent.) He thought LSD might be used to unearth the original fear. He warned that any treatment using LSD would need to be done in hospital. Dr Matthews then made a surprising change of direction:

> 'Hypnotism has been said to be very useful, but I have no experience of its value in this condition. If you considered this form of treatment you would be well advised to consult a really first class psychiatrist in London before doing do, in order to be sent to the right person. (There are hypnotists and hypnotists!) Dr Stafford-Clark of Guy's Hospital (who is the 'Consulting Psychiatrist' on the 'Lifeline' TV programme) is an extremely sound authority on these matters ... Think this over.'

I was a bit unsure about Dr Matthews' suggestion and needed some outside advice. So I wrote to a former teacher and now friend, David Lepine. He had left the school – which, pleasingly, he now referred to as 'the old cabbage patch' – to become first organist and choir master of the new Coventry Cathedral. He was someone I trusted and who would not beat around the bush. I told him I wanted to see the psychiatrist Dr David Stafford-Clark at the York Clinic. David replied with a typically outspoken, thoughtful, long and chatty letter:

> 'Don't give up about the stammer – press on. In this day and age it MUST be possible to cure it. Try every bloody thing – hypnotism – the lot. I've got a lot of faith in what the York Clinic does. After all, your stutter is a pretty mild one so it shouldn't be a great trouble.'

I was not too sold on that 'pretty mild one'. It did not seem so mild from inside my head! Anyway, my next in-for-a-penny letter was to Dr David Stafford-Clark himself. I had already come across his name. At school I had tried (and failed) to read his best-selling *Psychiatry Today* – one of those trusted blue Pelican books that appeared on the shelves of the school library. In those days he was a rarity: a psychiatrist who became a BBC television celebrity. He was known in the newspapers as 'the BBC's psychiatrist' – as if Auntie Beeb ever needed a psychiatrist!

His several series of BBC *Lifeline* programmes, which he wrote and presented, aired between 1957 and 1962. They were about psychiatry, the mind and new knowledge about the brain and memory. The 1961 the series included seven programmes about the 'unconscious'. In one programme a hypnosis researcher

– introduced simply as the 'Doctor' – and Stafford-Clark gave instructions to four already hypnotised subjects. For example the female subject had to answer questions about an imaginary visitor 'sitting' in an empty chair. I think one of those *Lifeline* programmes on the unconscious was the one I watched at home with my mother. I do not think my letter prompted a reply from Stafford-Clark. But I did get a letter from his research colleague Dr Stephen Black – he was the 'Doctor' who had appeared in that *Lifeline* programme. Dr Black suggested I went to see him. So I did. As I write, I have no idea at all what I expected to happen.

Who was this Dr Black? With Irish heritage, he was born in England in 1912. He went to university in Germany – leaving when Hitler came to power. During the war he worked for the Ministry of Health and then studied medicine in London. Once qualified, he concentrated on research. He worked alongside Stafford-Clark at the York Clinic. This clinic, which was opened in 1944, inherited much of its approach from its treatment of servicemen suffering from the trauma of war.

I knew virtually nothing about Dr Black when I turned up at Guy's Hospital in the summer of 1961. Sadly my memory of the visits to his consulting room is woefully incomplete. I think I had four appointments with Dr Black. I have no idea whether my mother knew about this treatment. I assume she did, even though I was by then nineteen. And I have no idea whether Dr Black charged for my treatment, or whether it was under the NHS. Or was it, perhaps, *pro bono* as part of his general research?

Before we get to my time with Dr Black, I need to explain briefly why hypnosis had suddenly become a fairly well accepted part of medicine. Hypnosis has a pretty dicey past – as Dr

Matthews had warned 'There are hypnotists and hypnotists'. In the 1890s Sigmund Freud gave up on hypnosis and instead launched psychoanalysis onto the neurotic world. In the 1920s and 1930s hypnosis was a staple of slightly more upmarket music halls. But during the 1950s two famous cases of treatment through hypnosis and then acceptance by the British Medical Association, gave it enough endorsement to allow the BBC to explain hypnosis and its uses in medicine.

In 1951 an anaesthetist called Dr Albert Mason used hypnosis to partially cure a young lad of a terrible congenital skin disease. Then in 1958 Stephen Black and Mason reported in *The Lancet* Mason's treatment by hypnosis of a woman with disabling hay fever. She was completely cured over a series of weekly half-hour sessions. In Black's book *Mind and Body* (1970), he details many cases of allergy patients he cured '... purely by hypnotic suggestion that they would not react allergically to the same stimuli in future.'

Whatever the state of the scientific investigation into hypnotism in medicine, I was not about to play with any dark arts or bogus people. I do recall being very nervous indeed when I first went to the York Clinic – a very Utility-looking six-storey box of bricks that had been shoe-horned into side streets around Guy's Hospital. In the first session, Dr Black asked all about me and told me all about himself, hypnotism and the unconscious mind. I cannot remember whether I told him that my father had stammered –- I must have done –- surely? He wanted to make sure I was a suitable patient, so towards the end of this session he set about hypnotising me. I vaguely recall that he was only fairly successful at my first session. He very probably asked me to relax a bit — relaxing was obviously still part of the solution to my problem. Not a good start to what I felt was the last chance to rid me of my wretched stammer. During the second session, while I concentrated on the tip of his shiny ballpoint pen, he succeeded in sending me into a hypnotic trance.

To bring patients out of a trance, Dr Black used the waking routine developed by Albert Mason:

'One, two – starting to wake; three, four – lighter and lighter; five, six –   coming out of it; seven, eight eyes open; nine, ten – wide awake.'

That sequence, which now seems rather corny, I remember as though it was used on me yesterday. In his book, Dr Black added: '...but if the subject fails to respond, the "learner hypnotist" may be in trouble, especially if he has a train to catch.' I do recall clearly that once 'wide awake' again, I remembered some of what Dr Black had been telling and asking me while I was hypnotised. But it soon faded – as fast as a bad movie fades from the memory. It must have been during my third session that Dr Black asked me when I started to stammer. 'When I was born', came the very clear reply.

On waking, I found Dr Black in a very skittish mood, rubbing his hands together and beaming: 'Well now, Anthony, do you know what you replied when I asked you when you'd begun stammering? You said, "When I was born"'. 'Yes,' I said, 'I remember saying that.' 'But that's nonsense, isn't it? No one starts to speak as soon as they're born – let alone to stammer. You've given me a classic Freudian Slip ...' And he summarised for me, in a very bite sized resumé, Freud's concept of the unconscious and wrote down the book he wanted me to read: Sigmund Freud's *The Psychopathology of Everyday Life* (1904). I duly bought it and read it. I have to say I found it hard going. Although I enjoyed the examples he related. Though he told a good story, I don't think I quite got my head around Freud's overall concept.

Then Dr Black asked me a very leading question: 'Why did you say 'when you were born' – what happened at your birth?' So I had to tell him.

I was a war-baby, born in a hospital in Salisbury, Wiltshire that had been taken over by the military. My birth was pre-NHS and not an Army perk – the bill came to £39 (nearly £2,000 in today's money.) My mother's recent illness – whether polio or the initial bout of MS – had left some of her important muscles too weak to attempt a natural birth. So I had a caesarean birth – attended by an army surgeon. This army surgeon was, in my mother's words, 'much the worse for drink'. And in helping me out of my mother, he managed to cut me – a fairly long gash along my right temple. My entry into the world at war was marked by a good deal of unnecessary blood, a row of stitches and I am sure lots of alcohol-fuelled cursing. In a certain light you can still just see the remains of the scar today and for years it featured in my passport under 'Special Peculiarities' (stammering did not count!). Thankfully, the surgeon was not allowed to do the repair. I bet it was left to a ward sister or matron who knew a thing or two about neat stitching.

Dr Black was delighted with this tale. His words went something like this:

> 'It's quite clear you were not too keen on entering this world
> – with such a bloody welcome you would have preferred to
> go back inside the womb – safe from careless scalpels –

and your stammer was a reaction to your precarious and probably very painful birth. We shall have to explain to you that there is a lot to explore in the world – much that is good and beneficial to you and a lot to take pleasure in.'

Dr Black was not an expert in stammering or speech therapy. But in *Mind and Body* he gave examples of stammerers he had treated with hypnosis and 'age-regression':

'I have regressed three overtly right-handed deep trance stammerers to the day when they "first learned to write" and found each of them anxious, or even agitated with an imaginary pencil in the left hand and apparently being instructed to use the right. It is a well-known neurological belief ... that one cause of stammering is the interference with brain function involved in being made right-handed when we are born left-handed.'

There was no such obvious cause for my stammer. As my father had noted in one of his wartime letters from France, I was plainly right-handed from the day I first wielded a crayon and scrawled riotous 'letters' to him. Although the key time might well not be writing as in writing words, but in holding a pencil and scribbling – copy-cat writing. But 'age-regression' had revealed one perfectly understandable cause. Dr Black was keen for me to leave any thought of returning to the womb well and truly behind me. His theory – which was quite new to me – had certainly convinced me. At my final session with Dr Black, whom I liked very much and with whom I was getting on really well, he went to town assuring me that there was a great deal of my life that was positive and I should seek out and relish fresh fields and those ever greener pastures new – especially now I was going to university. I am uncertain whether I was still in a medium trance or whether he was summing up after he had woken me up, but I clearly remember him telling me to make sure I started enjoying myself and urged me to start discovering 'girls' bottoms'.

Now that was pretty darn startling. Certainly not a phrase I had heard at home. Those were two words I had not heard spoken together during any of my many previous experiences of therapy for my stammer. Not just startling, it also set me thinking. The good Doctor Black had clearly spotted that my stammer and consequent anxiety about initiating conversations, seriously hampered my relationships with friends – and especially with girls. It looked to me as though Dr Black was onto something very worthwhile. I did tell my mother about my visits to the York Clinic – being, of course, careful to skirt round the bit about 'girls' bottoms'.

Dr Black was worried that I had not had quite enough sessions to cure me. So he taught me how to self-hypnotise. Doing this could, apparently, bring – without outside help – reinforcement of all that he had told me while I was under his hypnosis. It seemed very simple. But without his reassuring presence, I found the prospect of trying it truly alarming. I can now admit that I only tried it a couple of times. I became very worried that I would forget to wake myself up or forget how to wake myself up – or, worse still, could not wake myself up. Was that an opportunity missed?

Dr Black's treatment did not turn me overnight from introvert to extrovert, or from stammering to fluency. Yet it certainly provided a major step forward. Suddenly I was not stammering so much and was able to open conversations more easily. And that continued. I was, however, soon to discover there were still limits to my new fluency.

I am going into some detail about hypnotism and its medical uses at around the time I was treated by Dr Black, because I need to try and understand whether he improved my stammer as a physical symptom (of something much deeper) or did he merely give my ego a boost (low self-esteem being one probable underlying ingredient of the stammer – part of that ongoing 'mess'.) Did I set too much store by Dr Black and the tip of his ballpoint pen? I can see now that he was a really interesting scientist with wide interests whom I would have liked to get to know better.

Wondering recently about Dr Black's treatment and its effect on me, I have found out more about him and about hypnosis as part of medical treatment. It is most probably research I should have done much earlier.

From his various writings and later interviews, I get the feeling that Black's former colleague Mason held views of hypnosis as a way to treat medical conditions tended toward the sceptical. In 1964, he (with a colleague) published the results of experiments showing clearly that hypnosis did not stop messages of pain from a pinprick on the hand travelling to the brain. The brain was merely being told not to react to those messages. Of course, if it was only affecting symptoms not causes, these experiments had serious implications about what hypnosis could and could not do in treating most medical conditions – and stammers.

In 1960, Mason wrote that he had been unhappy some 'cures' were down to the 'great' self-deception of patients 'through motives of hope or even gratitude ...' He thought hypnosis had often been given 'a cloak of science':

> 'I have been even unhappier to see patients I have 'cured' of one symptom develop a second soon after, occasionally even worse than the first. The self-deception of doctors can also be great.'

It is not much of a surprise to find that Mason gave up on hypnotism, emigrated to the USA (where he had been born) and, following in Freud's footsteps, turned, very successfully, to psychotherapy. In an interview in 2011, he explained:

> 'I gave [hypnosis] up because I realised I was just relieving symptoms, and not giving the patient understanding. So, naturally they were reverting and relapsing and that's how I started to become an analyst.'

Also on the negative side is a much more recent opinion of Black given by Professor Heinz Wolff. Professor Wolff was (like Black) a research scientist and radio and television broadcaster. His career centred on bioengineering – a term he had coined. He had invented several new and life-enhancing medical gadgets. Here is Wolff speaking in 2014 about the Medical Research Council (MRC):

> 'In the 1960s the MRC at Hampstead got involved with a hypnotist called Stephen Black. The hypnotist initially performed quite well – he could for instance suppress an immune reaction that you got from vaccination merely by hypnotising people. He had subjects that were very sensitive to hypnosis ... but he blotted his copybook when he claimed to be able to hypnotize seaweed, which

was stretching people's comprehension a little, and then disappeared.'

Wolff was right about one thing. Dr Black had 'disappeared'. When he was 60 (in 1972) he retired from his Psychophysiological Research Unit, left his much-loved 500-year-old house at Lower Beeding in Sussex, and emigrated to New Zealand.

Dr Stephen Black's granddaughter, Julia Black, told me recently: 'Stephen's dream had always been, from my conversations with him, to have his own medical practice. It was always talked about as a positive move and one that he never looked back on. He said to me that he had never been happier than when he was practicing as a community doctor.'

Dr Black, his second wife and new young family settled in Bay of Islands in Northland – the subtropical area at the northern tip of North Island. There he built the Kawakawa Medical Centre. He died in Northland in 2006 aged 94. I should add that I have found no reference to Wolff's weird story that Black claimed he could hypnotise seaweed. I suspect it was nothing more than a pretty insulting scientist's in-joke.

Black may have 'disappeared', but unlike Mason, he had not abandoned hypnosis. In 1986 he published a paper in the *New Zealand Medical Journal* titled: 'Hypnosis in general practice'. It is a broad introduction explaining how hypnosis can be used and why it can be successful. From my own perspective this paper is of special interest. He refers to his success in curing a sixteen-year-old Northland boy who had suffered a brain injury that had led to neurological problems affecting his ability to swallow:

'However, this treatment involved 78 hypnotic sessions over six months ... The hypnotic treatment throughout was basically no more than direct suggestion: the patient was told that he would be able to swallow normally in future and that every day his swallowing would improve. A complete cure was effected.'

Perhaps my measly four sessions with Dr Black were simply not enough. Perhaps I should have persisted with Dr Black and his hypnosis.

6.

SATURDAY NIGHTS AND SUNDAY MORNINGS IN NOTTINGHAM

What kind of a person was I when I started at Nottingham University? I was definitely still a late developer – still a bit behind the curve. I am certain this was mainly thanks to the 'mess' surrounding my early life and my stammer. But I did now have a new vitality following that 'best ever' (as I assured my mother) speech therapy experience courtesy Dr Black's hypnosis.

I looked back on a varied childhood. It was certainly not Holden Caulfield's 'lousy childhood' with 'all that David Copperfield kind of crap'. At the other end of the scale and despite living in very rural Surrey, my childhood did not seem to me to have been full of Dylan Thomas' '... young and easy under the apple boughs about the Lilting house ...'. I certainly wasn't '... green and carefree' nor did I run '... my heedless ways.'

Now, with university a matter of days ahead, I felt a new

independence. What others saw in me at that time was another matter entirely. Would the relief of not stammering so much last? Would my stammer allow me to negotiate successfully this new independence, the new ways of learning and of making friends. Would my stammer, however much improved, allow me, please, to stop being such a solitary person? Looking back, I believe that between them my 'gap year' and Dr Black had cheered me up, allowed me to turn a corner. The 'mess' of nurture was becoming a bit clearer now the stammer was less apparent – most of the time. Would the hypnotist's skirmish with my stammer make seminars and tutorials possible – even enjoyable?

The first weeks as a student were very scary. So many people needed to know my name and all about me – from tutors to lecturers, from bookshop managers to fellow students. I found I was stammering rather too much. Then there were my digs. They were a change of buses away from the campus. Without, for the first month, a season ticket, each journey brought two 'discussions' with a bus conductor. The digs included some meals *en famille* – not, I can assure you, on the Eva Ducat scale. The man of the house was a retired and crotchety electrical engineer who thought he knew the answer to every problem and that conversation meant an endless series of barked questions – each one requiring not simple yes or no answers – but descriptions and justifications of student life and 'all your so-called work'. It was hard pounding and not good for the stammerer – he clucked loudly every time I got stuck. His wife was a gentler person and did not turn a hair at student mishaps.

My first foray into student life was with the Nottingham Everyman Club – a town and gown drama group. They were planning a production of *Dark of the Moon* – an Appalachian Mountain version of *The Ballad of Barbara Allen*. I was billed as co-producer with Brian Clark, who took the lead part opposite Val Deans. He was a mature student and a contemporary of mine in the English Department. He was a former teacher and seasoned actor who went on to write the very popular play *Whose Life is it Anyway?* I did not enjoy this producing/directing experience. I simply did not have the theatre experience to make the job enjoyable. But I was beginning to do some writing and was bucked when my *nom de plume* review of our production was accepted by the local newspaper – even though I included my own name in the review and said it had been a delight to watch. I was learning about newspapers! I did go on to produce and direct Samuel Beckett's *Krapp's Last Tape* with Donald McIver. Directing this was like having a long conversation. Inspired by Arnold Wesker's Centre 42 project to spread culture beyond its normal elite audience, we took it to the university's agricultural college – and we got an audience.

Later, Brian persuaded me to help him with the Dramsoc production of Bertolt Brecht's *Life of Galileo* – which had a huge and overwhelmingly male cast. I was billed as Assistant Producer, but also had two small 'walk-on' parts. One involved the tricky task of robing a Cardinal on stage. The other part was easier – I was the lovey-dovey partner to a young and very fair maid in a big crowd scene. Two *very* non-speaking parts. Once again, this production was not a happy experience. There was a day when Brian could not make an important rehearsal and it was left to me to get on with it. Trying to control the large cast of older egos and wavering first-time-on-stage actors, I stammered so much that the rehearsal ended rather abruptly. That aborted rehearsal really soured student drama for me and showed clearly, stammer in mind, that theatre was not likely ever to be a suitable career choice for me. I don't think I let my mother know this. Pity – it would have cheered her up no end.

I thought my spare time would be better used writing for the student newspaper – *Gongster* – and eventually editing the termly literary magazine *Gong*. Despite Dr Black's beneficial effect on my stammer, writing came more easily than talking.

The actor John Neville had just arrived at the Playhouse and most of Nottingham was waiting for the new Playhouse to be built with him as its first director. Every fortnight or so there was a must-see play at the old Playhouse. Neville as Macbeth, a revival of *The Caretaker*, Behan's *The Hostage*, *A Man for All Seasons* and so on. In between there were a couple of lively Jazz and Poetry sessions. Reviewing one of these for *Gongster* – I fell into a trap that would dog my life.

I had joined the dedicated band of student journalists quite early on, but only became deeply involved in – obsessed with? – journalism a bit later. John Neville was invited to give a lunchtime talk in the students' union. He took the opportunity to pour scorn and derision on student behaviour and student journalism and in particular on my review of his first jazz and poetry evening. He derided my implication that Carl Sandburg (born 1878) was one of the Beat Poets who came out of San Francisco in the 1950s. To make my review fit the page some of my words had been edited out – leaving the daft error of equating Sandburg with Allen Ginsberg and co. The trouble was that I was just not prepared to stand up and explain what had happened – for fear of a major stammer episode. So I just blushed a deep red and hid my face in my hands, as the audience laughed at my expense.

This episode confirmed for me that I was still unable to stand up and speak in public. Not you will note 'speak <u>fluently</u> in public ...' but to speak at all in public. I simply could not take the risk. The odds on the gamble were too short. This frustrated me to the point of depression. John Neville's showboating was quite easily forgotten. I even got over the disappointment of the *Galileo* debacle. But this limitation on public speaking really hit home when it came to politics.

At the start of our second year – October 1962 – the student body was engulfed in the Cuban missile crisis when the world really did stare oblivion in the face. Or so it seemed. Hour upon hour hundreds of students met in the Great Hall amidst heated debate to pass resolutions calling for the abandonment of nuclear weapons, calling on statesmen to save the world, to stop the foolish game of chicken and the madness of mutually assured destruction. I had argued against nuclear weapons with a one-time (brief time) girlfriend. Jane pulled no punches in arguing in favour of nuclear weapons. She was gorgeous with fine ash blonde bob, was quietly serious yet smiley and softly spoken. Her great advantage was that she ignored my stammer. Perhaps that allowed her to defeat me in argument on any topic we talked about. This she did – with a smile and a kiss. Her disadvantage was that she was the great niece of a fierce and gossipy elderly lady who lived just up the lane from us. So I had to be very careful what I said and how I behaved. Jane became a solicitor. On the evidence of her debating style, once in court she would, I am certain, have 'turned over' many opponents.

Also anti-CND was the student I had shared those digs with during my first year at Nottingham. Colin had even organised a pro-nuclear weapons march to London from his school in Sussex. So my arguments against the bomb had been carefully honed in many late night discussions. However, I avoided all those noisy student meetings. It was simply too frustrating not being able to stand up and take part. That frustration meant I passed through three years of university without participating in any politics at all. It was certainly not that I lacked political views, they were too obviously trumped by my stammer. Feeling excluded did hurt.

On the other hand, my stammer had very little impact on the academic side of university life – the 'work'. I did once ask a lecturer to excuse me from reading some Middle English text aloud (shades of junior school). But our course was mainly lecture-based with regular seminars – in which I did not participate very often – and tutorials. With just a tutor and one or two other students I was fine and fairly fluent. In my final year I did have to read a chapter of my dissertation to the tutorial group – its title was *The Political Style of William Cobbett*. I had a long-standing interest in Cobbett who was born near home, in Farnham, Surrey. This reading aloud worried me deeply and for several weeks I became very nervous and hardly slept. So I plucked up courage and asked my tutor if I could record the chapter in private onto my tape recorder and play it back when the dreaded day arrived. Being a really sympathetic and friendly man – from time to time I used to babysit his small children – Jim Boulton agreed. However, this only made my stammer more obvious to the other students who were faced with the unusual sight and sound of my tape recorder sitting beside me on a chair and at best an uneven reading performance. Even in the quiet and privacy of my own room, the tape recorder and its microphone were an audience too much. The chapter I chose to read in the tutorial began with three easy words 'For too long ...'. Then I hit the tight 'Will' of William followed by the impossibly hard 'C' of Cobbett. Hopeless combinations. Was Dr Black's influence beginning to fade?

We had started our three years of English Literature and language without a professor. James Kinsley (who took over from Vivian de Sola Pinto) was ill and his arrival was delayed to the start of our second term. Within a matter of weeks I was sitting in his room interviewing him for *Gongster*. This took me to another part of 'the mess' or nurture that was responsible for my stammer. My level of anxiety in front of people of authority, seniority or fame, almost always led to a severe bout of stammering. One of my worst moments occurred during a university vacation when I met Samuel Beckett at a party in the village. He was a cousin of the mother of one of my closest local friends. I was absolutely speechless. Not that I didn't have a lot to ask him. I just stammered. My interview with Professor Kinsley went somewhat more smoothly. He also cheered me up by acknowledging that Nottingham's very active student union probably led to less good degree results: 'But that's not,' he told me, 'wholly a matter for regret.' Professor Kinsley would rather see a good experienced citizen looking for a job than someone with a first and no outside interests or experience. Most reassuring!

Editing the termly literary magazine *Gong* was rewarding. I got to talk to people I would otherwise have never even met. I also got to work with many like-minded people – several of them natural writers and journalists. I did not have to speak at the launch of each term's issue – there was no launch party. We just went to the pub and sank a long glass of relief. Bliss.

Much of my writing was for the weekly newspaper *Gongster* and it included comment columns, features and above all the editorials. These were often written close to deadline – and sometimes so close that an editorial would be edited on the stone at the printers. We did not just send off a package of typescripts and hope someone would make it all look readable. We – Chris, George, Brian, Joe, Colin, Paul, Alan (later a professor of English at Hull University) and others – went over to an extraordinary workshop of expert printers at Ripley in Derbyshire. There we were allowed to learn on the job – often working on the stone with them. It was still the hot-metal era and I can still taste the smell of it.

Most of my editorials were quite short and punchy. But some, when I got the bit between my teeth, grew and grew. These longer editorials ensured the lead printer would put on his spectacles and peer at the type on the stone: 'Too long and too small to read. Make it shorter. But you won't will you!' – and he'd laugh. 'Students! You'll learn.' I really enjoyed writing those editorials and found that so long as I kept reading the newspapers, chatted long over coffees, and spoke quietly to some of the more open and enlightened members of the teaching staff, I had enough information and varied views to write sensible opinion pieces. Some of my friends told me they were just 'opinionated'!

How was the stammer affecting my social life? Although my attempted liaisons at Nottingham were not at all successful, they made me realise that I could just about cope with relationships despite my stammer. But could girls cope with my stammer? That remained a constant fear for me. The most caring of my unsuccessful paramours had an extraordinarily high quota of empathy that often fought with her somewhat heedless attraction to more than one man at a time. Ann once described herself to me as 'a most unrealistic female'. In my diary I described her as '... magnificently attractive. There is something Vitti-ish about her open faced smile'. I recall taking a huge gamble and asking her to my home. My idea was to take her on one of my favourite walks – to Puttenham Common a couple of miles from home, where Aldous Huxley set the dramatic ending of *Brave New World*. It is a finale quite unsuited to the purpose of our walk. Luckily we never reached that ill-fated spot. Her visit passed in a blur of anxiety.

The walk was followed by a pop-in visit and cup of tea to meet my mother and aunt at home. A good stiff whiskey would have been more appropriate. In retrospect this visit had not been a good idea. Ann had had the least stable upbringing one could imagine. She had survived it, but it still tore at her. Our relationship could be described in one word: angst. After teas and a chat, we then set off back to London. On the way, she told me that my troubles stemmed from a sort of split personality. I had, she said, one persona at home and a very different one at university. She said she was never sure which me she was meeting. Then Ann smiled her lovely, slightly naughty smile and added: 'But never mind. The really nice thing about us is that that you hardly stammer at all when you're alone with me.' Eventually, after too short a time and some very long and emotional letters, she told me 'it' could never happen. That was anguishingly that. 'I want you to forget me entirely'. Fat chance. I never really learnt why, but at least my stammer was not to blame.

I was leaving Nottingham without a job to go to, without

really a definite idea of what I wanted to do or what my stammer would allow me to do. My dreaded degree *viva* was a formal affair. The level of my degree was obviously plumb in the middle of the range – an Upper Second (aka a 'Two-one') that was clear of slipping down to a Two-two, but was well clear of the exalted First. So, despite the gowns and ties, it became a chatty affair. There was one question about my dissertation on William Cobbett. Then I was asked whether I had enjoyed working for the student newspaper and magazine? I said I enjoyed writing more than talking. Smiles all round. What do you want to do after this? Journalism. One of those taking the viva was George Hibbard – a great Shakespeare scholar. His lectures had been the best of the lot – he spoke with a lovely country accent and had a wonderful sense of humour. 'Ah,' said Dr Hibbard, 'I know just the place for you to start your journalism. The photocopy of that very interesting pamphlet you wrote about was bound into your dissertation upside down! You should work for *The Guardian* – they have a reputation for making all sorts of printing mistakes.' General laughter – and I was dismissed.

As well as being a somewhat worrying cliff edge, leaving Nottingham was a real wrench. Whatever the stammer-induced problems, however many girlfriend problems I had failed to solve, they had been three really happy years. The happiest years of my life – so far. The most obvious plus had been the new ease I found in making friends. Leaving these friends was a wrench. Although there are good friends made at Nottingham who are still our friends now – too many have died too young. Of course, some of these friendships have not lasted. I was friends with the university's resident artist, New Zealander Bill Culbert and his wife Pip. They had come to Nottingham via the south of France, and introduced me to cooking with olive oil and lots of vegetables. They invited Rosie and me to suppers and we stayed on playing Kiwi rules pontoon into the small hours. Rosie is still a good friend of ours. There was Philip who became a well-known barrister and married Barbara who is also still a good friend of ours. Philip died much too young. Chris was a stalwart of *Gongster* and *Gong*. He joined the *Manchester Guardian* and came with it to London. There were two Pauls – one became a well-known sociologist, the other a well-known and popular journalist. There were Clare, Heather, Rosemary, Angie, Christine and Judy. There was Ray Gosling who I persuaded to write for *Gong*. There was Peter and there was George. There was also a very lovely young woman who I had only been brave enough to ask for a very occasional coffee in the Student Union, but who would soon make an astounding change to my life.

I am getting ahead of myself. As I drove away from Nottingham I was thinking about other people and my uncertain future. In the haphazard way of things, with me on the homeward journey was the lanky form of Colin with whom I had shared those first digs. He had been up all night and slept most of the way south. Over our three student years I had bumped into him on *Gongster* business, but I did not know him much better than during that first term. As we neared the place at which I had agreed to drop him and his suitcase, he woke up: 'Thanks for the lift, Tony. That's been a real help. By the way, your stammer's so much less noticeable than when we were at those strange – very strange – digs in Bridgford. Well done – well done too for *Gong* – and good luck to you.' And he was away to thumb a lift home to Chichester. He went on to become a big noise (sound?) in commercial radio.

7.

EARNING A CRUST –
FIRST STEPS

When I left university in the summer of 1964 I did not know where I was heading.

George, with whom I had worked closely on *Gongster* and *Gong*, had decided to join the fairly new journalists' training scheme, which involved time on a local newspaper. We had discussed this option at some length. George (he was the George from Bolton whom I had first met at Oxford) would try to convince me to take the plunge and join the scheme. I would ask if he could guess my reaction at being told by some ink-stained news editor to beg, borrow or steal a photo of the young child just killed in a heedless road accident. Or I would tell him that I could not see myself knocking on doors, asking questions at crotchety press conferences, telephoning uncooperative people for information they did not think I should have, and – above all – having to phone in my copy to grouchy copytakers. They would, I explained, certainly gib at a trainee with a stammer.

I must add here that our long standing friends George and Peter (who stayed on at Nottingham to do a PhD), both died much too young.

For a career, I wanted the less public and quieter, behind the scenes, life of magazines, newspaper features or analytical articles and leaders: writing not talking. I needed no speaking in public and less speaking to the public – let alone to important public figures whose very presence would trigger instant stammering. Deep down I knew that to jump straight into that part of journalism was a tall order. But writing was a strength I could use. If I could find the right way to use it.

Phone-phobia – which had not been sufficiently quelled by Dr Black – meant that calling organisations and trying to find the right person to ask if I could come for a job interview, became a new nightmare. It led to procrastination (and still does so). I was better at writing letters. One of my letters appealed to Geoffrey Cox, then editor of Independent Television News (ITN). Perhaps it was the slim folder of cuttings from *Gongster* and the zany cover of one of my *Gong* issues that caught his eye. On the appointed day, I turned up at ITN's Kingsway headquarters. Geoffrey Cox appeared to be totally unaware of my stammer and put me at ease with a chatty interview about university and what I thought of his news organisation. But he had no vacancies and said he would keep my letter and papers on file. With his slight New Zealand twang, he wished me well. 'Hope to see you here sometime,' he said, and as he shook my hand he added with a smile, 'Perhaps when you've a *little* more experience in your folder.'

At this jobless moment in my life, the lack of a father was featuring quite high on the list of daily problems. First, he would have had clear views forged by his own experience as a stammerer, on how, when, where or even whether my stammer mattered. He would also have had contacts and friends to advise me. Besides, I just missed having a father.

My first job fell into my lap – courtesy the lady who had supplied *Gong* and *Gongster* with the national advertising that had kept us afloat financially. Someone had asked – with great urgency – whether she knew of a likely recent graduate to join the London operation of an American television news film agency called United Press International Newsfilm (UPIN). I drove to its UK headquarters at the Rank Film Laboratories in Denham for an interview. The following Monday I started at UPIN on the night shift. Yippee – I had a job. What I could not have known then was that I had also chanced upon the beginnings of a career.

For me UPIN was an ideal introduction to a small corner of the world of television journalism. Almost all the communication with the outside world was by written messages sent mainly via UPI's agency newswires. Towards the end of the night shift we sent an 'advisory' for clients so they knew what newsfilm was on its way to them by airfreight – yes, airfreight! We typed the advisory punching it onto many-holed 'ticker-tape' and before long, I could read straight off the tape – though not quite as fast as the teleprinter or the Telex machines did. For a stammerer it was a dream way to communicate.

Sometimes we actually got to go out on a local story. My first assignment was Sir Winston Churchill's final days. On cold January nights, I sat in a film cameraman's very draughty sports car parked at the top of Hyde Park Gate – the small street where the Churchills had their London home. Any sign of anything stirring around the house, of anyone arriving or leaving at any time of the night, saw a flourish of cameras. It was enthralling, if also very cold and left me feeling a bit of a 'rubber-necker' (a term my mother often used with emphatic disapproval). All I had to do was to summon up the courage to ask other journalists the names of those who were coming and going.

Away from work, my newly independent life saw me sharing a flat in Earl's Court with some friends. I met up with many other friends for evenings out and, once I was working shifts, during the daytime. It was almost like being a student again – with the fun side uppermost. On 23 January 1965, Rosemary, a friend from Nottingham, had a small party at the flat she was sharing in west London. I went to the party briefly before my night shift began, and once it was over, I hurried back to the party – returning by 4 am. My diary's two-line entry ends: 'Long chat with Al.' Reminding her of this, she mentioned that the flat was so short of chairs that during the 'long chat' she sat on my lap. 'Al' was Alison Clarke. I had known her at Nottingham as someone beyond my reach, except for those occasional coffees. She was amazingly beautiful. With lively blue eyes. An unmissable smile. She was and has remained level-headed, fun, funny and wondrous.

Right now, I rather regret referring to the stuff of nurture and the context to my stammer as 'mess'. This was not mess at all. This was simply wonderful, enchanting, captivating and intense. I took her to see NF Simpson's hilarious play *One Way Pendulum*. Did we laugh till we cried? I cannot remember – it was all too delicious. This liaison, this meeting was so different to my trail of ill-judged infatuations and often rather obsessive attempts at relationships with unattainable or uninterested women. From the start, we seemed to be utterly compatible. This was meant to work for us both.

My diary for that year was not a work of record – let alone a work of art. It usually consisted of a couple of phrases and sometimes even a whole sentence. But on 21 April 1965 it went into overdrive:

> 'Take Al to The Bull's Head (Mortlake) [a favourite jazz venue] – afterwards we decided we wanted to get MARRIED. I have never felt so sure and marvellous ... It has such enormous future implications. The FUTURE suddenly becomes full of everything gorgeous – so much to discuss with Al who is so so super-Al.'

Right from our first meeting, I was certain Alison simply felt the stammer was nothing more than another part of me. She never questioned my stammer or commented on it – unless I asked her opinion. Nor did her family. Suddenly I had found a future that made sense, replacing in one fell swoop the old future, riddled as that had been, with doubts and uncertainties.

While the better part of my life started here, Alison is a name I still find very difficult to say. So, *only as regards her name*, this was not the best laid of plans. In every other way it was a fresh start to our lives. But from the off, my most obvious failing in the partnership was my repeated failure to introduce Alison by her name. Instead, going against all my intentions and principles, I would be left saying 'And this is my wife ...'. To make polite and appropriate introductions, a name is vitally important. 'My wife' implied some crazy sort of ownership – not what I intended at all. On better days I could sometimes manage 'This is my wife

Alison' – a 'slide-through' word. But the merger of sounds did not work often enough. When I flunked it, Alison would then have to jump in with a smiling 'Hello, I'm Alison.' This left me feeling woefully unhappy. We have had a mutual support pact. But she has taken a far greater proportion of the supporting than I have – quantifiable in the thousands of phone calls she has made for me and unquantifiable in the major amount of talking she has done for us both. Of special note is her willingness – when my courage to make myself understood over noise and bustle forsakes me – to struggle to bars at innumerable crowded events to order drinks and food.

One way out of this name trap was to stick to her widely used nickname – Al. As in Paul Simon's haunting – for us – 'You can call me Al'. 'Al' I can manage perfectly well. I should add that at university many friends started to call me Tony and once I began working, the Tony stuck.

We defied parental advice and got married just a year and six days after we had clicked, just before dawn at that party. We had a parent-pleasing church service with – as I have mentioned a sympathetic clergyman – Rosemary's helpful father. Wonderful. We have lived and loved together through the thick waters of political turbulence and the thin air of dying family and friends.

Oh – and at 8.30 am on 24 January, Sir Winston Churchill died. I was due on shift that Sunday. With such huge international interest, the abnormal number of film stories that night was daunting. My diary has one scribbled line: 'One bloody hell of a night.' I seem to recall it was one of the nights when the laboratory manager succeeded in getting very drunk. He found it hard persuading his team to work through their meal breaks so as to get this great pile of newsfilm clips onto flights out of Heathrow. In case that last sentence sounds silly, we should remind ourselves that this was the pre-satellite and pre-digital era when the news cycle was more penny farthing than super bike.

The decision Al and I had made to marry as soon as possible, meant that unremitting night work looked ever less appetising. My diary is filled with the detritus of job hunting. I even tried to get an interview for a job at *Vogue* – through a contact of Chris, ex *Gongster* and our 'best man', who was by then securely ensconced at *The Guardian.* At least this shot in the dark led to a very posh lunch with a truly lovely and helpful young Irish woman called Polly – and an invitation to a party she was giving. It was a good party, but unsurprisingly, for many long weeks no job materialised.

Jobs number two and three both ended suddenly when my stammer became too much for my bosses. Too much what? Too embarrassing for them, too much of an interference in my work … just too much? I worked in the Central Office of Information's Television News Unit – a place where news really did morph into propaganda. Whereas UPIN had been a good place to work with a stammer, the COI was very different. My main problem became the telephone. I worked in a small office with three other people. And, overheard at such close range, I found cold calling companies asking to borrow their film and photographs or fix interviews very difficult indeed.

My first filming venture for the COI was to publicise British merchandise being produced for the 1966 World Cup finals. At the Design Centre I filmed captain Bobby Moore looking at the items and trying some out. I then had to do a short on camera interview with Bobby. He was just the nicest, gentlest, most understanding and helpful man. But, despite his help, my interview produced only two short usable soundbites from him. Not a huge success. But I did do better on other projects. Then, out of the blue, in July 1966 I had an appraisal with my boss – Arthur. He said outright that with my stammer in its present state I would not be able to move on to more interesting television work in his department or any other part of the COI's Film and Television Division. The job search began again.

My first port of call was BBC News. I got as far as sitting a test, but then learnt that in those days, the BBC's newsroom journalists read their draft stories aloud to typists. So that ruled me out. Then I got a phone call from UPIN – they were merging with ITN's syndication service and wanted me back as a day editor and there was talk of big expansion for the new UPITN agency. I jumped at the offer.

This job gave me extensive experience in how to edit newsfilm for television. Often done at great speed to meet a deadline, editing from camera rushes to give the sense of a narrative or of occasion was a great skill. And the ITN film editors who worked for UPITN were real experts. Working beside them in an edit suite and helping to choose shots or a 'soundbite' was an amazing education. I also learnt how to make instant judgements about what could and what should not be shown. That was not just to do with the amount of blood on show – a more difficult area as we moved from black and white into colour. Some freelance cameramen in Asia felt the need to linger on sights unfit for most front rooms.

The main way newsfilm was delivered in Europe was changing fast. The developing daily electronic Eurovision News Exchanges became the main means of distributing agency newsfilm to major clients. Decisions on what stories would feature in each day's News Exchanges were made during daily morning audio circuit conferences linking agencies and broadcasters right across Europe. This was a serious challenge for me. Just answering the register of attendees was difficult enough. I found explaining the niceties of a film story offered for a News Exchange awkward – sometimes more than awkward.

I felt this was becoming a significant problem. I had seen a television programme that mentioned a weird metronome that produced a 'superimposed rhythm' to help produce speech fluency. In 1830 someone invented this version of the metronome especially for stammerers. It was called, believe it or not, the 'orthophonic lyre' and looked very much as though it was designed to resemble a table ornament. I asked my brother-in-law, John, if he could create a mini electronic gizmo that could produce similar metronome-like clicks to give my speech a helpful rhythm. He was then a lecturer in electrical engineering and is now an archaeologist. In no time at all, he made me a splendid gadget that fitted into a small carton – once home to a pack of playing cards. At the flick of a switch it produced a rhythmic clicking that I could feel, but was too quiet for anyone to hear. It proved an excellent aid to formal talking – such as reading offers on the conference circuit. I had not foreseen the problems of using it for general conversation. For a few months I used it a lot. Then one day I put it back in the jacket pocket where it lived, and promptly sat on my jacket. A sad end to a worthy experiment.

There came a day when Simon, one of UPITN's three senior journalists, said he wanted to stretch his legs and have a smoke, would I go out for a short walk with him? I did. He had bad news for me. The boss, a shy and rather secretive man called Ken, had made it clear that UPITN was not the place for me and I would get no promotion – because of my stammer. Simon was very apologetic and made it very clear it was not what he wanted at all. But Ken was in charge.

Once again it was time to look for another – and more suitable – job.

8.

AT ITN – 'PLEASURE WORKING WITH YOU, SIR'

Rescue came with a surprise job offer from Independent Television News. Hugh, ITN's managing editor, came downstairs to the UPITN newsroom: 'Can you come and have a chat? Is this a good time?' It had to be a good time. We went to his office and, there and then, he offered me a job as an ITN writer. He then took me to the Editor's office and I was introduced to Nigel Ryan. That was it – done and dusted. I shall never know whether UPITN's boss or Simon asked ITN if they had a role I could fill – perhaps to avoid the awkwardness and expense of UPITN having to 'let me go'.

On 1 January 1973 I began at ITN. Four people joined the ITN editorial team that day: Trevor McDonald (from Trinidad via the BBC World Service), Arthur Maimane (from South Africa via BBC Television), Sam Hall (from Reuters) and myself. One general reporter –- Trevor –- and three 'writers'. ITN was a can-do organisation with a big budget and big ambitions. Some of its confidence must have rubbed off on me for my stammer became much less of a problem. Anyway, no one at ITN seemed to notice it.

Entering the world of broadcast news was both thrilling and intimidating. My first week there was filled with trepidation and apprehension. I quickly learnt that most newscasters had their own style. Working on the lunchtime bulletin, Robert Kee would glance through my written words, put a line through them and write his own more colloquial version round the edge of the paper. At the beginning of July 1973 I was made a Deputy Chief Sub. David Nicholas, then ITN's deputy editor, was keen to ensure that his programmes made the very best use of all the film and video available to ITN. So he invented a new job: Chief Sub Film. I was chosen to be the first one. As David put it: 'You're in charge of hoovering up the best pictures' – especially for the flagship *News at Ten*. Then came the 1973 Yom Kippur (or October) War. Coverage started flowing into ITN from a multitude of sources. That war increased my visibility, established my value to programme editors and gave me experience of economical and quick reel-to-reel editing (with ITN's expert technicians) on two-inch video.

After a few months, I did my share as ITN producer/fixer in Belfast – a fortnight at a time during some of the worst bombings and outrages. There was a contretemps over my stammer during one of my stints in Belfast. ITN's office was a shed on the flat roof of Ulster Television's studios – a fairly safe place as it usually had a discreet police presence nearby. The office had a phone line and a telephone answering machine to record messages and, most importantly, tip-offs. The message had to be a fresh one every day: 'Hello, it's Monday evening and this ITN's office in Belfast – please leave any messages for the reporting team after the beep ...' It was my job to record the message before we locked up for the night. This I usually managed without too much stammering. But one night I was very tired and nervous and it was awful. The film editor over from London was appalled: 'ITN cannot be represented by your message – it's ... it's not the right image.' He insisted I try again. And again. The more I tried the worse I got. He was not one of my favourite people. Occasionally ITN's quiet brand of exceptionalism came to the surface and caused aggravation. Eventually I asked him to record the message himself and I went off to have lots to drink with a friendly Northern Irish contact.

Without any fuss or palaver, I was asked to take on some shifts as day editor on the foreign desk. Being duty foreign editor presented me with a real hurdle. I had been to many morning editorial meetings with ITN's editor, the programme editors and duty news editors. I had heard how the home and foreign input editors described their offerings and logistics for the day ahead. The truly amazing thing about ITN was that no one ever complained about the way I stammered my way through the day's foreign news list. I made a point of starting early enough to write a very full and detailed summary of the day's likely stories and reports. I knew there were programme editors in the meetings who were itching to get down to the newsroom and start shaping their programmes. Their apparent decision to simply ignore my stammer, I found remarkable, praiseworthy and very supportive. If any senior producers ever made complaints about my stammer, I knew nothing about them and they must have been rebuffed higher up the editorial tree. I was working with some great journalists and, for the most part, with wonderful people. I remember with special affection political fount-of-all knowledge Julian Haviland, and reporters Jon Lander, Nik Gowing, Tony Carthew, Carol Barnes, Peter Snow, Jon Snow, Rory MacPherson, Desmond Hamill and Trevor McDonald. With special mention to three of those who were of great support to me: studio director Diana Edwards-Jones and unflappable newscasters Ivor Mills and Sir Alastair Burnet. All three 'characters' and friends.

I was duty foreign editor on some terrifying and notable news days – especially during the final paroxysms of the Vietnam War. It was a time when satellite feeds were not a matter of flicking a few switches and when film – black and white or colour – had to be developed at a laboratory before it could be edited and transmitted to London. I look now at my Foreign Desk contacts book and my heart sinks at the number of people I telephoned during those times to ensure ITN got its reports on time. ITN had a lot of clout, but the American nets had clout plus a money tree, and, thanks to their World Service, everyone wanted to help the Beeb.

There were times when my stammer could have had pretty disastrous results. One such moment came during the Watergate hearings. After the report of the day's cross examinations was fed in by satellite, I stayed in the Master Control Room during *News at Ten* talking on the sound line to the producer in Washington as he watched for late developments on the American networks' live programmes. I would then pass these by phone to the studio control room for a headline at the end of the programme. One night we hit a Watergate crisis point. I cannot remember the precise details. But for me it involved the stammerers' cherished thesaurus of synonyms that are easy to say – a vital (if many would say counterproductive) aid to everyday life. The producer said that someone important had been arrested. 'Arrested' was not good for me, so I told the studio he had been 'charged', which was easy for me. The Washington producer could hear me relaying his messages and screamed at me down the audio line: 'NO, NO Tony – arrested – he's not been charged.' Caught out and embarrassed, I quickly corrected it (well fairly quickly) and was grateful to hear the newscaster use the right words for the end headlines.

How did I feel about working in this high-pressure, highly skilled environment? What anxieties did I have to cope with each morning as I travelled in to start a shift? As well as the slowly diminishing fear of making a catastrophic mistake, my stammer left me with an almost permanent sense of trepidation. Sometimes the shock of breaking news came on a quiet evening on the foreign desk (a call from a friend at ABC News' London bureau: 'Tony? Thought you ought to know – Reagan's been shot – just heard it on our live link from New York.' 'Thanks so much – bye.') or it came at home ('Sorry to wake you Tony, John Lennon's been shot – he's dead.' 'Oh no, no, no.') You'd be hard pushed to stammer for a while after the adrenalin rush from that kind of call – even a couple of hours before *News at Ten* or at four in the morning.

There were some briefly embarrassing moments, which I simply put behind me and pressed on to complete the shift or the project. The Saturday 'lunchbox' bulletin, coming just before ITV's *World of Sport,* got a pretty good audience. One Saturday the Labour Party – in another of its well-worn crises – was holding a special conference. I was working a rare shift as Chief Sub – responsible for getting the bulletin off air smoothly and on time. At the conference someone was talking too much and the vote was delayed. So our bulletin was running long and there was no way we could meet the off-air time and include the vital, delayed result of the vote. I pressed down the key and started to talk to the *World of Sport* studio – asking for an extra thirty seconds. It was a bad stammering day. Back came a friendly voice – a lovely calm PA's voice – a Production Assistant who worked at ITN too: 'It's Tony! Don't worry, Tony, we'll just follow you off air – take your time!' It was Hilary. Crisis solved.

There was at least one occasion on which my stammer appeared to make a positive contribution to news gathering on the foreign desk. In the United States home-bred radicals had invaded a courthouse and taken judges, lawyers and others hostage. We had heard there had been a telephone interview with the leader of the gang. So I stayed on the foreign desk during the lunch break, got hold of the phone number and started dialling it. At that time our phones had no redial mode, but at least we were using buttons rather than painfully slow rotary dials. I sat and hit the buttons for ages to no effect. Then suddenly I was through. 'Hello,' I said, 'who am I speaking to?' 'The man with the guns'. 'Oh, I see. W-w-would you d-d-o an interview for B-B-British t-t-eevee n-n-news?' 'Hey, take it easy. Why are you rushing and stuttering so much?' So we got chatting. He had, surprise, surprise, a friend who stuttered badly. I told him I always stuttered and asked him very nicely to hold the line while I found a reporter to interview him. 'Hey. No hurry – I can stay on the line. I've got time – lots of time. There's not much happening here' – and he roared with laughter.

Who the heck was this guy? I was NOT going to interview him myself – however helpful he was being. Reporter Geoffrey Archer interrupted his lunch and reached the recording booth clutching a piece of Reuters copy and recorded an interview which made the bulletins. Should we have been speaking to him – giving him what Mrs T called 'oxygen'? In America they talk to anyone and everyone. I saw no reason whatsoever why we could not find out his side of the story rather than take the version being relayed to us from police and politicians. Anyway, he seemed very savvy and accepting about people with stutters/stammers.

You may well ask why on earth was I working in a job that required constant telephone calls to places that in normal life you don't expect to have to speak to and to people you have to persuade to talk to you and then to do you favours. There is a photo of the author standing by a paper strewn table in a temporary newsroom set up at NBC's headquarters for 'foreign broadcasters' during the 1980 US Presidential Election – Reagan's landslide victory. He is holding a telephone receiver to each ear and looking frazzled. It's such a pity the photographer missed his efforts to talk into three phones at once.

This was, I should note, the time when the coverage of international direct dialling was still expanding. There were still plenty of countries which you could only reach through London's international switchboard. ITN's switchboard – run by the redoubtable Jo – was of enormous help to the foreign desk and especially to me. They would often call up at the end of the day to make sure we did not need any difficult connections during the night – to New Zealand for instance. As well as help from the switchboard, I had hourly and daily support from the foreign desk's assistants: Barbara, Maggie, Jan, Sue, Angela and others too. Like Alison, they were quite prepared to help out with tricky 'phone calls. Lucky me.

The four-and-a-half months during which reporter Michael Nicholson, cameraman Tom Phillips and sound recordist Micky

Doyle, were missing and out of touch in Angola during its complex civil war, have left indelible memories. Those months involved endless phone calls from the foreign desk to people who said they knew all about UNITA, Jonas Savimbi, the MPLA, the Cuban troops, the South African involvement, the Soviet Embassy in Luanda – even about the country's fauna, flora and likely landing strips. There were also daily calls to the wives and families of the missing reporter and crew – offering all manner of assistance to their stress-filled lives. These were often the hardest calls of the day. ITN was excellent at looking after people. But sometimes close relations just wanted to be left alone. They did not want to be reminded of the fear they were living with.

After a dramatic rescue from Angola by chartered jet, I received a letter from ITN's editor, David Nicholas. This is not an autobiography and I am congenitally unhappy about boasting. But this letter helps to show why I felt so at home at ITN and how my stammer was never part of my ITN equation:

My dear Tony,

I find it difficult to express how much ITN and our team in Angola owe to you for what you have done.

I appreciate the colossal strain you have been under. But I would like to say that your contribution to the rescue, your tactful and sensitive handling of the domestic problems, and the not insignificant matter of running a foreign desk in the meanwhile have impressed me deeply.

Pleasure working with you, sir. Yours ever, David

I read an obituary the other day of a former ITN journalist. It included a phrase which made me sit up. He was, the obituarist wrote, 'a diplomatic correspondent and a newscaster for ITN during its heyday in the 1970s.' Such 'heydays' meant that working at ITN gave you not just confidence, but a certain status. Often with three or four *News at Tens* in the week's top twenty most viewed television programmes, people in Britain knew you mattered – and very often wanted to help. This status or added authority was also good for my stammer. ITN carried a major helping of authority, and as that authority passed through to me – however far down the pecking order I was – it really did help my fluency.

1977 was my big year at ITN. I was appointed producer for ITN's coverage of Queen Elizabeth II's Silver Jubilee year. This involved a lot of travel at home as the Queen made her triumphant tour around all four nations of the Union, and abroad as she visited Germany, Canada and the Caribbean. I was working with a reporter I liked and admired – Tony Carthew, who used to sign off his reports with a crisp 'Anthony Carthew'. We had serious times marvelling at the size and enthusiasm of the crowds and also a lot of fun. We guessed the time of the first sighting each day of the inevitable pack of Brownies, we second-guessed the colour of the Queen's outfits and wondered about the age of the Lord Lieutenants at each stop. Pairs of Brownies held hands securely and giggled, hoping no doubt the Queen would wave to them. Her Maj (pronounced, I'm afraid, as 'Madge') had not been Queen for 25 years to suddenly start ignoring girls in uniform – as she once was herself. (I never joined cubs or scouts. Too much stammering involved.) I always got the colour of the Queen's outfits wrong. I was clueless on Vogue-type shades and styles. The Lord Lieutenants always looked old, their worrying eyes scouring the scene to see what might go wrong.

We had an excellent journalist assistant: Laura got me out of many pickles and was brilliant at persuading important people we were not the BBC, but they should help us anyway. The year also involved some scary moments. Especially when the meticulous planning of Royal events went awry (often because of the size of the crowds that came out to see the Queen – as they did for the lighting of the Windsor beacon), or when broadcast trades unions got in the way (and we were reduced to a single camera outside broadcast unit at Buckingham Palace), or timing delays (like the much-heralded, very delayed evening balcony appearance with the Royal Family apparently sat inside for what seemed to me like an hour, watching ITN's single camera zooming slowly in and slowly out again, while Alastair Burnet adlibbed for them and ITV viewers, a learned, detailed and colourful history of balcony appearances, the Palace and much else besides. Extraordinary.)

The year ended with ITN's hour-long, prime time documentary review of the Jubilee year – *Jubilee: A Right Royal Celebration*. This programme, which I produced, netted a handsomely large audience for ITV. During the year we had extraordinary freedom to cover what we thought the audience would appreciate and also to take a slightly caustic and unwishy-washy view of some of the events. The only time ITN's editor intervened was over one commentary line in the documentary. Carthew was asked not to say over a shot of Lord Snowdon standing on the steps of St Paul's Cathedral with children David and Sarah, that it was 'his turn to have the children' – he and Princess Margaret had separated the previous year. I did not bother

March 1942: the family together in Salisbury - Andrew
aged eight, Anthony aged a few weeks

Late May 1944: Lt Col CG Millett and Anthony at home in Elstead

Circa 1949: young
Anthony Millett

Below : 1963:
Anthony Millett –
student journalist
at Nottingham
University (Photo:
Haydon Luke)

4 November 1980, New York: Tony Millett (right) in ITN's Presidential Election newsroom at NBC's studios

1935: North West Frontier, India: Capt George Millett (front and centre) with men of his 1DCLI Company

2 April 1941: King George VI watches training somewhere in Southern Command. CGM (second left) holds the King's greatcoat. (© IWM H8657. War Office photographer: Lt EG Malindine)

28 July 1944: medal ceremony for 3rd Division – General Montgomery meets officers commanding 185th Brigade battalions at Chateau Cazelle, Normandy. Lt Col Millett is third from left. Second from left is Lt Col Bellamy (DCLI colleague & CO 1 Norfolks). Right with back to camera is Major-Gen Whistler 3rd Division's Commander.

(©IWM A 70 136-6 (film still))

December 1944: Lt Col CG Millett's grave in Venray – soon after his funeral

1992: Alison Millett

Below: 20 December 2014: Thomas at Venray's Commonwealth War Cemetery

to try and change the editor's mind.

Carthew was a great reporter. It is best that I quote the former colleague of ours, Trevor McDonald. When Tony died, Trevor wrote to me:

'I believe that Carthew's style was such a part of what we all once boasted ITN was all about – to the point, elegant and graceful. He was such a marvellous writer and I remember when I hesitated on being offered an ITN job by Nigel Ryan, he suggested I should talk to Tony Carthew, who Nigel felt represented all that was best about the firm. He also singlehandedly changed the way Royal reporting should be done.'

I think I had got through that whole year without being depressed about my stammer or feeling my stammer had interfered with my work.

The Queen's first stops on her long, winding and crowd-filled UK tour had been in Scotland. In Edinburgh, after watching the Royal Company of Archers doing their bit as the Sovereign's Bodyguard, I took an hour off to go to the Stammering Research Unit at the city's university to collect a piece of equipment I had agreed to use as part of its initial trial. One more attempt to find some way to overcome my stammer.

It was the Edinburgh Masker. This consisted of a throat microphone held in place by an elastic ribbon, a gadget that slipped into a pocket, small headphones and associated wires. The idea was that as soon as you started speaking, a hum was fed to your ears so you could not hear yourself stammer. And that, it said on the tin, eased or even stopped your stammering. I did warn them that I spent much of my time at work on the phone and did not see how the Masker would work with a normal telephone receiver clamped to my ear.

When I started to use it in the newsroom I found, as I expected, it was hopeless for phone calls. During normal chatter with programme teams, you could not hear when someone interrupted you – and there were lots of interruptions in a hectic and pressured newsroom. Above all, it was embarrassing to wear the equipment – and the band holding the throat mike in place was hot, sweaty and uncomfy after an hour or so. It was all the more embarrassing when some colleagues asked why I was wearing the thing as they did not believe my stammer mattered or affected my work – in fact barely acknowledged I had a stammer. I found I could not use it in morning meetings where it might have been most use – simply because I could not hear questions fired at me midway through my explanations of developing stories, satellite times and so on. In the end I felt that wearing the Masker highlighted my stammer more than it helped it or made it disappear.

I got many calls from the Edinburgh researchers asking for my opinion of the Masker and how much it helped me. In the end they got quite cross with me for 'spoiling' their trial. Although some stammerers – notably in the United States – have used it successfully as a 'crutch', the Edinburgh Masker is no longer available. There are, I should note, some newer electronic fluency devices using micro technology that may help some stammerers. (See stamma.org/get-support/apps-devices)

The Edinburgh Masker was my last attempt to do something serious about my stammer. From then on I would just have to make the best of it. That was not so much a decision, as simply the acceptance that I had been able to do pretty well with the stammer, so why not carry on doing so? Whether there was more to my decision than that I was not sure.

Apart from the really helpful feeling that I had the authority and status of ITN behind me, another way to ensure a period of slightly more fluent speech was to have a drink – or two. Alcohol, as too many have learned the hard way, is a disinhibitor. Certainly for me it can loosen something that helps my fluency. Not to be advised in most circumstances, but I have been known to resort to a quick swig of something before, for instance, addressing a hall full of international broadcasters at a Eurovision News Exchange conference.

There was a very generous culture at ITN. Ninety-nine per cent of the time everyone was working to the same ends. I would remember – very clearly indeed! – if anyone at ITN had ever said 'Can you cope with this?' or 'Do you want someone else to do that for you?' Ninety-nine per cent of the time my stammer's possible effect on my work was never questioned.

There were very senior people who simply ignored my stammer and gave me opportunities to expand the list of roles I could fill. Quite early in my time at ITN, I was on the foreign desk the day it became clear that President Nixon was about to resign. Or was he? His speech was due in the early hours of our 9 August 1974 – 02.00BST – and ITN had persuaded the ITV network to stay on air. This was the era well before 24/7 broadcasting and staying on air meant, we were told, engineers climbing transmitters to stop them switching off automatically. So quite a lot was riding on ITN's hunch that this was would be an historic address. David Nicholas asked me to produce the programme with Reggie Bosanquet presenting. Reggie was a newscaster and a character –

very popular with the audience. But often a wee bit unpredictable. I was brave enough to ask whether Reggie would be at his best at that time of night – and was assured he had promised 'to be good'. And indeed he was. Very good.

Being nominally in charge meant that my stammer disappeared for the duration. In its place was some extreme stress – was Nixon really going to resign? I held my breath during the first minutes of his opening waffle: 'This is the 37th time I have spoken to you from this office ...'. Jumping out of my skin when he said: 'I have never been a quitter.' About a quarter of his way through his lengthy text he finally said it: 'Therefore, I shall resign the Presidency effective at noon tomorrow.' Phew. A moment of history gone in a bundle of scripts and sweaty palms. After we came off air I rushed into the studio to thank Reggie: 'Glad to be of use ... what an extraordinary night! Well done.' It was Reggie who used to tease me gently about my stammer: 'Millett', he would shout across the newsroom in the general direction of the foreign desk, 'Don't look so damn worried. As soon as we get those hour long news programmes, they'll let you be a newscaster.' It was a good joke and went a long way to easing the pressures I sometimes felt.

Then, in 1981, I decided to leave ITN. I have frequently asked myself why on earth I chose to leave a leading – *the* leading? – news broadcaster which seemed oblivious to my stammer. It did feel that I had reached as high up ITN's editorial structure as I could expect to go. My very own 'glass ceiling' feeling. Some friends from UPITN (including Simon) were setting up an independent television production company specialising in news – Television News Team (TNT) – and I joined them. Let's just say that we underestimated the continuing strength of the unions and the need to hire a single top-flight programme maker. We survived for a while and in some months we flourished.

Apart from being a director of the company, I hired myself out to the winner of ITV's new breakfast franchise, TV-am. At first I was a consultant on foreign news and then, when things came badly unstuck a few days after they went on air, they wanted me to be Head of News. TV-am was a maelstrom of egos and blithe promises. Strange to say, I do not remember significant interference from my stammer. Quite the contrary. Having a title and a management role seemed to give me enough authority to quell the stammer. I even went to argue with the man from London Electricity who came to cut off the supply when TV-am's ongoing crisis lurched into a cash crisis. I also tried to dissuade my friend Anna Ford from spilling some beans to the press waiting eagerly outside Egg-cup House – I failed. I had great support from the people who had been recruited as oversight directors of TV-am News to give the new broadcaster some 'balls'. These supporters included Sir Geoffrey Cox and a charming man at the Independent Broadcasting Authority, David Glencross. The IBA's reputation was on the line as TV-am started to run rings round the promises on which they had won the franchise. These people now helped me defend the standard and depth of the news agenda as it was being diluted to make way for light entertainment material. My time at TV-am ended when the new management was firmly entrenched and they did not need a Head of News who believed in serious news values, but wanted one keen to tell TV-am's smallish audience about Diana Dors' dieting successes.

I tried to get by with freelancing, but found the stammer

getting in the way. I was simply no good at selling myself. Proof of the continuing influence of my stammer, came when, as a freelance, I produced a report for Channel 4 News during the miners' strike. I had found a mine in South Wales that had used inventive new methods to prove it was still sitting on top of huge and accessible reserves. This posed questions for the Thatcher government's view that British coal was getting too expensive to bring to the surface. Worryingly, there was no reporter available to accompany the crew and myself to South Wales. So I had to do the interviews myself. This was not successful and shocked the rather po-faced ITN cameraman. I very much suspect he told his bosses that he would never again take me on a story as reporter or interviewer. However, the report itself – voiced by a newscaster – was a success.

Stewart Purvis, whom I had known during my earlier years at ITN and who had been made editor Channel 4 News charged with saving it from embarrassing failure, asked me to be the programme's first Foreign Editor. I willingly gave up freelancing and rejoined ITN on 1 January 1985. My years on Channel 4 News were something of a roller coaster – with many more highs than lows. To begin with there was a definite antipathy and frostiness shown to me by those who had been in at the start of the programme in November 1982.

But things got better. The occasion when I showed that I could shout down a telephone line as well as anyone else, probably helped. We had asked Channel Four for a short extension to the programme to include live coverage of Ronald Reagan signing a very important nuclear treaty in Washington. I arranged with ITN's engineers to get a cheap-as-possible satellite feed. Sure enough you get what you pay for – the quality of the pictures was substandard. So much so that Channel Four's chief engineer asked the Post Office Tower switching centre to let him 'see the feed'. This vague question prompted someone to switch the feed to Channel Four's technical suite at their headquarters and our broadcast coverage of the signing went to black. After much screaming we got the feedback – in a matter of seconds. As the programme came off air and with the whole newsroom in eager earshot, I phoned the Chief Engineer at Channel Four. I told him in no uncertain loud and stammer-free terms that unless the channel gave the programme a proper budget, there would always be a danger we might need cheap-as-possible video feeds. It was way above my pay grade to say so, but Stewart was content as I was supporting his pleas for a bigger budget.

From being Foreign Editor, I moved up to Programme Editor – and once again felt the slings and arrows of outrageous jealousy. It was almost as though a person who stammered should not get that kind of promotion. I may well have misread the reason for the antagonism – stammering can make you a bit paranoid. This job meant I had to take the morning meeting. After a few months, the Channel 4 News team were getting used to me. One morning the Home Desk found a story about penguins. Penguin chocolate biscuits were then being advertised ad nauseam with the 'Pick up a P-p-p-penguin' slogan. When I reached this cod story in my run down, I duly obliged. Cue much laughter. All good clean fun.

I am rushing through my time on Channel 4 News solely because there was not a lot of stammering worth noting or commenting on. I had great support from Stewart, from the programme's next editor Richard Tait, from Sue Inglish and from correspondents and reporters including Edward Stourton, Anne Perkins, Trevor McDonald, Jon Snow, Judy Aslett, Alex Thomson, Michael Crick, Gaby Rado, Fiona Murch, David Smith, and the incomparable Elinor Goodman. And keeping the foreign desk together Angela, Helen and Jo. Richard sometimes asked me give the 'post-mortem' talk to the staff at the end of a programme. Mine were, despite some hesitations, mercifully short, allowing staff a bit more of their evenings at home.

From programme editor I was moved up to Editorial Manager. I recently found the letter detailing my job spec for this post. I am quite surprised I agreed to take it. The spec details a daunting amount of logistics work beyond my competence. I was appointed just in time to organise the programme's move to ITN's brand new and swanky building in Gray's Inn Road. This was a chore that ran from choosing desk designs to making decisions on technical things I never expected to have to understand. No sooner had I got the whole team installed in our pristine and roomy newsroom – with unprecedented elbowroom, legroom and swung-cat room – than the building's spiralling costs nearly brought ITN down. As the crisis unfolded, we had to move into a newsroom that was not much bigger than the old one and was below window level. How they all loved that. How they all blamed me.

My main memory of those years is that I played – despite my stammer – a full part in the senior editorial team. For example, when a crisis arose over Channel 4 News' access to South Africa, I went with David Nicholas, then ITN's Editor and Chief Executive, and Trevor McDonald to the South African Embassy (as it still was) in Trafalgar Square – a grand imperial redoubt of a building. We had managed to get Trevor a working journalist's visa for his second reporting visit to South Africa. This was timed as serious preparations started for the release from prison of Nelson Mandela. Then the visa was suddenly withdrawn – we thought it was a decision made in Pretoria rather than London. At the meeting, I remember holding forth to Ambassador Dennis Worrall (who had made several visits to our studio for live interviews) on the rich and varied agenda of our reports from his country – many of them looking on the more positive side rather than merely the demonstrations and violence. I was lucky. The meeting in the Ambassador's office overlooking the Square was held against the perpetual chanting of anti-Apartheid demonstrators standing just below his office windows. Weird as this was, it helped my fluency – it was rather like having the Edinburgh Masker blotting out my voice, so I just kept talking. Or was I taking advantage of the difficulty many people find in interrupting adult stammerers? Probably. There have to be some pluses.

After a pause to make it look as though they were ignoring our pleas, Trevor's visa was restored. I should add that two years after I joined Channel 4 News, my own application – of course as foreign editor rather than reporter – for a visa was also rejected by Pretoria. They had 'previous' – and perhaps found, deep in their archives, that I had 'previous' too.

I also enjoyed managing the other Channel Four programmes that ITN provided. I even enjoyed the daily Parliament Programme which always teetered on the verge of financial bankruptcy, although its team was the opposite of bankrupt – chock full of good (and often expensive!) ideas. We worked with some amazing people: Sue Cameron, Nick Woolley, Sarah Baxter and Sir Robin Day.

Eventually it was thought that I should move on from Channel 4 News. The Channel's movers and shakers liked newness and shaking people up with newcomers. On 30 November 1993, Stewart – now ITN's Editor-in-Chief – made me Editor, International News Programmes. I was in charge of ITN World News with its new and lead contract to supply news for the American network NBC's Super Channel satellite service across Europe. I really enjoyed this low-budget news gathering with some great journalists and technicians, and with some top-line presenters including Richard Lindley, Selina Scott and Mary Nightingale. Though it became a bit wearing trying to convince senior NBC executives that ace reporter Richard Lindley was not 'too British' for the channel's European viewers.

It all came unstuck with the appointment by Michael Green of ITN's new Chief Exec. He came from *The Economist* and knew nothing about television, but knew he had to find profits for Mr Green. He set about making impossible cost paring demands on our World News service that was covered by a watertight supply contract. To add injury to insult during an in-house display of new voice activated studio equipment, I had taken the system's designer and its salesman aside to ask how I might be able to use it. Unfortunately, the Chief Exec overheard me, picked up on my question in front of the full panoply of ITN's senior managers, senior journalists and senior engineers: 'Yes,' he said to the salesman, 'that's a good point. Tony has a *very bad* stammer – how could he cope with this gear?' Time to go.

9.

GENES ... AND JEANS

My working life after ITN – what there was left of it – had very little to do with my stammer. It did not feature very much in the short time I was at Reuters Television. Though there was one dire occasion during a presentation to a roomful of senior and diehard Reuters Television people. That brought concerned questions from an old UPITN friend who was working there: 'Matey, that was not even your usual standard. Oh dear. Anything wrong? Can I help?' No – not really. Just woefully let down by a sudden bout of inferiority in the face of such a senior – and obviously hostile – crowd of nincompoops. Sickening.

I then tried to freelance in a consultant sort of role. This took me for the first time to the BBC – to BBC World. I did not enjoy freelancing. Quite simply, selling oneself is not something that comes easily to a stammerer. I soon came round to thinking I was just about old enough to retire or at least to take a ninety degree career turn.

I went as a very mature student to King's College London's War Studies Department. I wanted to research a PhD on British war crimes policy that led to the Nuremburg prosecutions. My interest arose from delving into the bizarre war crimes trials held at the end of the First World War, which I had come to via evidence of the brutal killing by occupying German troops of a British soldier who was being hidden by a French family near Le Cateau. Until, that is, he was betrayed, in story-book fashion, by a 'woman of ill repute'. As it was thirty years since I had last attended university, they first made me complete their one-year taught MA course. This was like being back at school – a very high-powered school. It involved a number of dicey duels with my stammer. I had to take part in discussions and deliver a tutorial and more. There was even something that seemed very like the dreaded reading round in class.

After the MA, the research for my PhD became an almost wholly solo enterprise – involving trips to archives here, there and everywhere. Most enjoyable – and very largely stammer-free. My viva was, to my immense relief, a chatty affair with the charming and sensitive senior lecturer and Professor Mark Mazower, a renowned international historian whose work I really admired. The kick in the teeth came when I answered the department's call for volunteers to teach young students. I said I could not stand in front of a lecture hall full of students, but I could teach and run discussions with small groups. Reply came there none.

I must own up that I very seldom use my 'Doctor' title. This is not because I fear being called to attend a mid-flight heart attack. It is simply that the D for Doctor can still stop me in my tracks.

Having retired from that academic life – a second retirement – my next sortie into the world of journalism was in Wiltshire. Alison (also with a PhD and after her very successful career in education) and I could now both tick all those boxes that say 'retired'. She worked for a local charity and I got back into journalism with a new news website for Marlborough and its surrounding villages. I enjoyed it. But still found telephone interviews something I would rather not even try to undertake. While I still have to fight the urge to postpone tricky phone calls to people who do not know me, my stammer now has far less impact. It is more at ease with life. It had, after all, generally been much more of a public stammer than a private one.

In the past I have dived hastily into arguments, without thinking about my stammer. Sometimes it works. I once, while pitching for work for Television News Team, had a terribly loud argument over lunch with someone who defended the Apartheid regime on the grounds that South Africa had such wonderfully beautiful landscapes and wondrous flora and fauna, which, she claimed, trumped the country's appalling politics and dreadful inhumanity. Weird logic or illogical weirdness. Fuelled by anger at her stupidity and a glass or two, I unwisely countered by extolling the extraordinarily beautiful countryside and so on in so many parts of the Soviet Union. She nearly bit my head off: 'But they're Communists.' A TNT colleague sitting beside me, turned and whispered: 'Tony, you're not stammering – keep going!'

Shortly before the COVID-19 pandemic hit Britain, I made a third retirement. I resigned as a director of marlborough.news and stopped being a journalist. The end of a satisfying and, I hope, a useful career. Satisfying despite my very own glass ceiling.

Why then was my time at ITN the best of times? There were no other major stammerers there. Arthur Maimane had a slight hesitation in his speech. Reggie Bosanquet had a faint and slightly slurring version of the traditional lisp (which some people mistook for him being a bit the worse of drink – which he very occasionally was). That committed and sharp reporter Sue Lloyd-Roberts had a fairly pronounced lisp, which in the eyes of a very few unnecessarily critical people diminished her journalistic worth. How wrong they were. Sadly, she died much too young.

One of ITN's favourite and most brilliant freelance cameramen, Nairobi-based Mohinder Dhillon did have an obvious stammer. He had mostly learned to overcome it – primarily by speaking very softly. He always addressed me – whether on a crackly phone line from Kenya in the middle of the night or in person at ITN – as 'My friend Tony'. With the easy-for-him 'my friend' allowing him to slide into the difficult hard 'T' for Tony. He died in 2020 and his obituary mentioned his 'very severe stammer'. That shocked me as I had never thought of it as that much of a problem to him. I was also shocked to see how old he was – he was 88 when he died. He was a true gent with an eagle eye for catching details with his camera.

And while we are on speech patterns, I should mention that one of ITN's best journalists had voice difficulties. He did not stammer, but his delivery was unusual – so much so that although ITN was spending a significant proportion of its overseas budget keeping him in the Middle East, one producer of *News at Ten* simply refused to run his reports. I recall sitting with David late into the night in the Meikles Hotel in Salisbury (now Harare), trying to persuade him not to give up and to find someone who could iron out his delivery. At least he saw the funny side of a friend with an obvious stammer who could never make a broadcast reporter, trying to help out with his speech problems. He was

certainly determined and was for a long time Channel 4 News'
very successful correspondent in Moscow and then Washington.

———————————

British television has not been very kind to stammerers. I found
two popular programmes particularly galling. One of *Call My
Bluff*'s team captains was the Irish journalist Patrick Campbell
(actually 3rd Baron Glenavy). He had a conspicuous stammer.
Television audiences seemed to overlook the stammer and were
delighted by his Irish wit. When 'locked solid' at the start of a
word he would, apparently, hit his hand on his knee and mutter,
'Come along! Come along!' I am afraid I could not face watching
Campbell stammering to make us laugh. Being able to see his facial
distortions and frustrations made it much, much worse for me.

In 1976, Ronnie Barker made his first stammering appearance
as the corner-shop owner Albert Arkwright in *Open All Hours*.
The stammer was not in the script for the first episode, but was
added by Barker purely for comic effect. This addition was not a
necessary or sustained part of the shopkeeper's miserly and fairly
bullying character. I found it grotesque and silly. It was not even
a very good stammer. It laid me open to a few people trying a
Ronnie Barker take-off in my hearing – to see if I would rise to
the bait. By that stage in my life, I found them easy enough to
ignore.

10.

FAMILY MATTERS

Have I concentrated in these chapters too much on the negative bits
– the bad news bits of my stammering life? I have simply wanted to
show how a stammer can – if you are not able to control it – influence
life choices, can restrict them and can rule parts of a stammerer's
life. By writing this I hope to make a small contribution to the way
stammering is viewed and understood. And, of course, to promote
the earliest possible and most up-to-date therapy for stammering
children. I certainly do not want anyone to reach the conclusion
that my life has been miserable – has been made miserable by my
stammer. It has not. No one could be miserable who has had a
lovely and wonderful wife for so many years, or has been fortunate
enough, as we have been, to have two such brilliant daughters, their
partners and our grand grandsons.

I do know that in these chapters I have concentrated too much
on myself. I have omitted consideration of the impact my stammer
has had on our family. I do fully appreciate that a stammer does
affect a number of other people – but especially close family
members. One of the advantages of working very long days at

ITN, fourteen or fifteen hour days (and sometimes more) on the foreign desk or as chief sub film, was the number of compensating full days off. This gave home life a very different feel. It allowed me to take more responsibility for daughters Susannah and Liza, such as taking and fetching from the local school. I trust I did not embarrass them too much when I was, on a bad stammering day, overheard chatting to teachers and parents. The long days off also allowed us to spend time with a growing number of friends. We had long, happy supper evenings, many outings and visits to Alison's parents and my mother and aunt and holidays abroad.

Of course our two daughters realised very early I had problems speaking fluently. But neither of them remembers any of their friends ever asking about or commenting on my stammer. Susannah has a very vivid memory of a bad telephone call the she could not help overhearing: 'I remember clearly one very difficult phone call – to South Africa I believe – that you had to make. Why were phones always in the hall in those days?' She also remembers me trying to prepare for a speech I had to make using 'that speech box thing' – the Edinburgh Masker.

'Obviously you found lots of situations and days at work difficult and I remember being aware that you were sometimes stressed and anxious – and also your frustration when things were tough. I also remember it just being normal. And not stopping you as you moved on and up. Both jolly good things to grow up around.'

That occasion with the Masker also features in Liza's memories of growing up with a stammering father. But she has a telling example of how my stammer helped her:

'One thing that has always stuck in my mind was my interview at Sheffield University. The chap had a severe stammer and really struggled throughout, but I remember how glad I was to be able to respond to the situation in the right way (despite my nerves!), to be patient, not interrupt or finish sentences for him – as I'm sure a fair few people did.'

Liza remembers some stressful times – and times I caused her some anxiety:

'Rather than specific events, I think my memories are much more around feelings and emotions, very much based around wanting you to be ok and to not have to struggle or get stressed because of it. Much more so, but not exclusively, in situations with strangers – restaurants, introductions etc. I remember distinctly feeling anxious for you, and often willing you with all my might to get a word out that you were struggling with – because I knew it was difficult for you and I wanted your discomfort to stop. Also, just to add that I always felt very proud of you, forging your way to the top of a profession where speech (and not a small amount of swearing!) was so integral – so easy to forget that all this was largely BE – Before Email!'

There – I am embarrassed again! I have made plain the enormous – absolutely unquantifiable – debt I owe to Alison for her long, patient and lasting support. But the impact of my stammer was not something she could always help with especially when it was far from positive in its effect on her:

'The sort of situations like introductions and ordering food and drink didn't cause me any problems – of course I didn't mind taking over. But I was aware of the embarrassment this caused you. The worst effect was the stress your stammer caused you – and how you reacted. You don't weep and wail, you tend to become irritable. And that's obviously difficult for me. So, times like the build-up to a foreign trip became stressful for me. You did get short-tempered – and I did not like that.'

From time to time that has posed some bleakish problems for us. Alison does not remember anyone asking questions about my stammer when she started going out with me or when we decided to marry.

'It was just part of you. What mattered to me was you getting upset. And if you were upset you did get irritable. But I don't remember feeling anything like shame that you weren't able to do things. I know I did sometimes finish words for you, which we're not supposed to do. But if you're ordering food or something it's just silly not to. At home and on holidays your stammer didn't really raise its head. Anyway, if we were in France I'd be talking to shopkeepers and waiters and so on.'

So much for my skills with the French language!

There have been rare occasions beyond newsrooms, edit suites and studios that have caused my family alarm and anxiety. I was once physically attacked by a taxi driver. Leaving ITN after a late transmission, I hailed a taxi. A driver stopped for me. Having stammered out my destination, I was getting into the cab when the driver jumped out, opened the other passenger door grabbed my briefcase and flung it onto the pavement. He then ran round grabbed me, pulled me very roughly out of the cab and flung me onto the pavement. I cannot be certain that he was upset with my stammer – perhaps he thought I was putting it on to rile him. Certainly at the time I was afraid his attack was the consequence of my stammering request. Perhaps he had a stammer or his wife had a stammer and, in an automatic response, he thought I was mimicking and mocking him. A bit unlikely. But people are known to believe a stammerer is mimicking them. In Hollywood, the actress Marion Davies had a terrible moment when she stammered while meeting fellow-stammerer Somerset Maugham. He thought she was mimicking him and apparently stormed off shouting at her 'Fre-fre-fresh b-b-b-bitch.' Perhaps in my case it was simply that the taxi driver did not want to take me to Clapham, thinking it was a bit too near to Brixton. Luckily I noted his Public Carriage Office licence number and, with a black eye, sore head and hurt pride, I went to the police. It turned out that the driver had borrowed a friend's cab. Quite against the regulations.

I mention this bruising incident because it shows how all-pervasive a stammer can be. It can foster in a stammerer the feeling that every disadvantage that crops up is down to his or her stammer. A stammer can from time to time promote a feeling of paranoia – and nearly everything comes back to it. Lots of things are against you – from menus that don't include ham salads to people answering your telephone calls with their hand over the receiver to bus conductors unwilling to wait to hear your destination. That feeling is inappropriate and has to be conquered.

Many, many years ago, a speech therapist asked me, out of the blue, whether I ever felt humiliated by my stammer. She was, I suppose, trying to establish my underlying attitude to the problem. I recall being very taken aback by her question. Apart from that awful Dale Carnegie evening, I think I was only ever humiliated when my stammer prevented me taking part in something I really wanted to be involved in – most frequently something political. That was not a public humiliation, just a bout of private angst at a decision I had made solely because of my stammer – often due to a lack of courage.

Early on in my life I had developed an attitude based on my perception that life was a sort of struggle – especially for me. In part this attitude may have been absorbed from my surroundings – life for my mother was, I realised early on, a struggle. She bravely faced up to her new life as a war widow with slim financial means. Before her illness made it impossible, she would bicycle over to a local hospital to mend their bed linen or to nearby villages to look after young children. I think she sometimes struggled with loneliness. She certainly struggled with her illness. Yet she never stopped keeping on, smiling and staying positive. My struggle was set fast in my stammer. However, the need to fight on does not mean you never smile, never laugh at a joke or never show enjoyment at being with a relation or friend. Yet it most certainly can lead to a view of the world about you and, more importantly, your place in that world, that is more negative than positive, more pessimistic than optimistic. Alison was my daily mainstay and our lively daughters were a great tonic and, as the phrase goes, certainly kept me grounded.

It may be thought that my stammer was nothing more than

a defence mechanism that I should have grown out of. Was I merely a shy kid with sticky-out ears who used the stammer as an excuse not to meet people? Someone will put their hand in the air and ask: 'Why didn't you get more advice about overcoming your stammer? Nowadays lots of people control their stammers – better than you do.' I can make a two track defence to that criticism. First, having spent too many hours in speech therapy that was for the most part simply wrong for me, I had given up searching for one that might work. I simply did not have the right level of determination. Or perhaps I should have been told much earlier in my life that there is no full 'cure' for a stammer. It has to be controlled.

Secondly, soon after university I reached the point where, stammer or no stammer, I had to carry on regardless – I had to earn a living. After two dead ends, I was very lucky to find an employer who seemed unfazed by my stammer and who put me in roles that I could fulfil quite well – even very happily and with some success. Perhaps it involved a split decision: half of me wanted to get rid of the stammer. The other half – the dominant half – just could not face the process of therapy and just wanted to get on with life and, as best I could, ignore the stammer.

I will always believe that the inherited gene made me susceptible to stammering – so I reacted to the trauma of my birth or the disruption of family life by war and illness with a stammer. However, it is important to know that recent research has discovered that stammering is not the province of any single gene. There needs to be an interaction between many different genes and the stammering may or may not be 'switched on' by issues in that messy area called 'nurture' – a child's development, their experiences, their environment and their temperament may all be involved.

There are a myriad of everyday instances that pass by quickly and certainly do not eat into the soul. One such is the fear that people are not talking to you and you cannot tell whether it is their embarrassment or yours that is uppermost in their minds. It was quite easy to become paranoid about this kind of speech hurdle.

There has been in recent years more attention to stammering – and this ought to be educating non-stammerers about the problems stammerers face. For many, *The King's Speech* was an eye-opener.

The distinction between 'private' and 'public' has always been important for my stammer. It is a distinction that goes a little way beyond the usual, straightforward meaning of those two words. For instance, it is crucial to acknowledge the difference between a private, informal conversation or chat and the more public nature of a phone call which can often involve not just the recipient (who may even have opened our conversation on loudspeaker), but also those nearby and listening to your side of the call. The former I can manage without a problem; the latter can induce serious stammering. It's very much the same with the problem of repeating a statement. I can often say something, however garbled or under-the-breath quietly, without problem. However, if it was too garbled or too quiet for the intended hearer, they will ask me to repeat it – and then I will often stammer quite badly.

I have needed – especially recently – to know more about the person my stammer came from. How had my father outfoxed his stammer? Through what hoops had he been with his stammer hovering about him like some interfering and ill-mannered sprite? His army career with its steady timeline of promotions, was not derailed by his stammer. How come?

PART TWO

11.

LIKE FATHER, LIKE SON – II

On 20 December 2014 three generations of the Millett family were in Venray to mark the seventieth anniversary of my father's death. It was the first time that both our grandsons had been old enough to understand the full meaning of this visit. It was a bitterly cold day – possibly as cold as winter 1944. After Venray's Commonwealth War Graves Commission cemetery, we went to the river in the area where my father was killed and later to the vast German war cemetery nearby. I have a photograph of Thomas standing on his own looking out over the neat rows of Venray's war graves – and thinking. Following my family's tradition of preferring silence to talk, I never asked him what he was thinking about. He probably was not thinking about his great-grandfather's stammer, but perhaps about the seeming futility of lives lost in war. For me it is extraordinarily strange to realise that neither of us, grandson and grandfather, knew the person who was buried there and can never know very much about him and his stammer.

Despite the family silence about his stammer, it is, unsurprisingly, the main reason I feel such an affinity with my father.

—————————

There is not a great deal of first-hand information about my father and his stammer. He is not even very visible in the family photo albums. There is, however, one very brief moving image of him. It is kept in the archives of the Imperial War Museum. Two War Office cameramen covered the occasion on 27 July 1944 in France when the 21st Army Group commander, General Montgomery (his promotion to Field-Marshal came five weeks later) presented gallantry medals to men of his old Division, which now included my father's battalion – 2 King's Shropshire Light Infantry. One cameraman was high up in Chateau Cazelle (then the HQ of 185 Brigade). The other cameraman, who was at ground level, captured the only moving image of my father I have found. My father is plainly visible in one brief shot. With Monty were the commanding officers of the brigade's three infantry and field artillery battalions (Lieutenant-Colonels Gibbs, Bellamy, Millett and Foster). In the chateau grounds, with brigade HQ troops drawn up on parade, Monty presented members of the Division with medals won on D-Day and during the long drawn out fight for the city of Caen.

Monty is introduced to the four commanding officers. And there is my father – waiting at the far end of the line to speak with Monty. He looks nervously thin. We do not see him talking to Monty. This was just two weeks after he had taken over as Commanding Officer of 2KSLI. George's mention of the event in that day's letter to his wife, Rita, was pretty perfunctory:

> Not very much news. Monty was here giving medals – in tremendous form. I think I got away with it for the time being!

He was sometimes unsure he was good enough for the job he had just been given – a not-too-serious case of 'imposter syndrome'. My father met Monty again in the week before he was killed and from that occasion there is a photo, signed by Monty, of him with my father and sundry officers – his friends.

Many years after the war and long before I knew of connections with my father, I remember seeing a newspaper photo of Monty walking to his local post office in Farnham to collect his monthly pension. I decided that I would go the following month and see if I could spot him. I did go and I did see Monty, wearing his army great coat and still sporting a black beret. He looked as though he was pleased to be famous, rather than the man of the people image he was intending to foster. I could have crossed West Street, stopped him and asked about my father. Would he, though, have remembered George Millett? Perhaps a senior officer with a stammer might well have stuck in his memory. Anyway, I would never have dared risk a stammering question to such an important person.

Where had my stammer come from? Dr Black's theory had not ruled out the likelihood that I had been born with a propensity to stammer – the rogue gene part of life. My father, Cecil George Millett (always known as George), had a stammer. That I know as fact. However, I have left it far too late to learn much about his stammer – how bad it was, whether he had therapy for it, how much it bothered him and how far it affected his life. At home and as I grew up, his stammer was simply never mentioned. In those days, I suppose, stammering was rather unthinkingly considered just another disability and generally disabilities were not mentioned. I have, as we shall see, two brief pieces of written evidence that my father not only had a stammer, but also that it stayed with him to the end of his life.

In general terms, my father's rise up the ranks to assume command of battalions shows that he made sure his stammer did not impede promotion – and to chart that success we shall, briefly, follow his career. There are some specific episodes that prove the point. For instance, there is his letter of 15 June 1944 – eight days after he went ashore across the Normandy beaches:

> Most days I hold a press conference (like Roosevelt!) I ought to have been a newspaper man – I can lie just as well as they can.

Some of this ability and determination to proceed without direct reference to or permission from his stammer would have come from his growing confidence. And in the armed services confidence can increase with promotion – indeed, it has to.

I have asked my brother about George's stammer. But he does not remember much about our father. Andrew is nine years older than I am and so had just had his eleventh birthday when our father was killed. He says that between his being at boarding school and my father being stationed away from home so much, Andrew seldom saw him and his memories of him are few and uncertain. Andrew certainly does not recall the stammer being a problem: 'I have no personal recollection of his stammering. Maybe I don't remember him stammering because he did not do it *en famille*. Interesting.'

I have found only one wartime written reference to my father's stammer. I have found no criticism whatsoever that his stammer undermined or inhibited his effectiveness as commanding officer in charge of some 800 officers and men. I did get to know two veterans who said his stammer never stopped him chatting with them or interfered with the minute-by-minute organisation of battle.

———————————

The early life of my father, Cecil George Millett was largely shaped by his parents' ages. His father, Charles Frederick Millett was born in 1838 – just six years after the Great Reform Act pushed Britain unwillingly into a pale and faltering version of our modern world. When he married Elizabeth Harcourt, he was 59 and she was 37. CF Millett was 65 when George Millett was born and he died aged 79 in the year George was 14. And George's mother died aged 64 in 1924 – when George was 20.

George was born on 8 April 1903. He had an elder brother, Charles, and a younger sister, Eleanor – known and loved as Nell. The family moved, probably after CF Millett's retirement as the London School Board's solicitor, to St Leonards-on-Sea. There they enjoyed the social life of Hastings and Bournemouth and of the Kent and Sussex countryside. I have no first-hand knowledge of their parents. However, from several spiky remarks made by my mother, I gleaned the impression that George and his mother did not get along very easily. I recall my mother referring to her as 'testy'. This has stuck in my mind because I was then young enough that I needed to ask what 'testy' meant.

For much of his life, George was obsessed by horses. He rode to hounds, he rode for the pleasure of riding, he played polo, he rode in cross-country steeplechases. He rode in Britain and in Spain (while he was stationed in Gibraltar). He rode a great deal in India – both on duty and off duty hunting jackal and playing polo. I do wonder how far this obsession with horses came about as a result of his stammer. As you ride, you can stammer away to a horse and it has no reaction to your stammer and there's rarely anyone close enough to overhear your stammering chatter. Your horse certainly won't laugh at your attempts to speak, nor will it blush with embarrassment at your efforts. It will certainly get to know the sound of your voice. Alternatively, some people with stammers find they can speak perfectly fluently to animals.

In passing, I should acknowledge briefly that those early parental deaths in the lives of Charles, George and Nell meant that my brother and I grew up without paternal grandparents and that my mother had no parent-in-laws to worry about. We had our mother's mother as an attentive if somewhat crotchety grandmother. She had been left on her own when her husband decided to live a separate life in Devon. He had taken off with the housekeeper of the country guest house they ran in the thirties. Just another bit of family 'mess'.

George was too young to serve in the First World War, but Charles joined the Royal Flying Corps and then, during the Second World War, joined the RAF where he stayed till he retired. Nell turned to farming – successfully – first in East Sussex, then in Warwickshire and finally in Devon.

With both George's parents dead by the time he was twenty, it is very tempting to jump straight from this woefully depleted family to understand why he joined that great family enterprise the British army. There he would find many lasting friendships and a busy social life. For officers, the British army provided a ready-made family setting as large as any civilian clan of friends and families. We should also note that this was still very much the era of Empire, and the British army was called on to travel to those red-coloured bits on the world map to keep them safe from those who – unsurprisingly – took exception, often violent exception, to British occupation. For a young man with a stammer, the army may have provided a ready-made family, but on the obverse of the King's shilling, it also provided many and daily hurdles and challenges. I certainly picture his army as a pretty hostile environment for any stammerer. As with schoolboys, men brought together in often extreme circumstances might be expected to resort to teasing a stammerer – even resorting to some mild bullying. However, King's Regulations required due deference and respect be paid to officers – even to lowly subalterns. So my father was at least spared open teasing from the ranks. In extremis, he had, I believe, more than enough skills and charm to prevent fellow officers making fun of his stammer.

After boarding school at Haileybury followed by Sandhurst, in February 1923, George was commissioned into the Duke of Cornwall's Light Infantry (DCLI) and joined the regiment's Second Battalion in Cologne as part of the Treaty of Versailles' occupying forces – the first 'British Army of the Rhine'. He had started his career as a professional solider.

Why did he choose that regiment? Quite simply because he was from a line of Cornish Milletts that has been traced back to the end of the sixteenth century. Many years earlier Milletts had come from France – perhaps enticed by jobs in mining or fishing and maybe as Protestants fleeing the violent antagonism of French Catholics. One line of Cornish Milletts hailed from the area surrounding the village of Marazion which lies a couple of miles east of Penzance. West of Penzance is the small town of St Just – there stood what my father referred to as 'the Millett house'. He certainly loved Cornwall and the Cornish – especially Cornishmen who served with his regiment. There is a small but very telling paragraph in a letter George wrote in January 1944. He had a good ear for the Cornish voice:

> Where I lunched there were two soldier waiters from the regiment [DCLI]. One from the 30th battalion said he had been batman to someone but 'he had left we'! Nice after all the tribal language I've heard for so long!

How I would love to have asked my father what precisely he meant by 'tribal language'!

In 1924, his battalion moved to the Channel Islands and then had a lengthy spell of home duty in Aldershot – 1927–1932. With defence spending at an all-time low, army life was fairly dull and, like many other units, the regiment and his battalion were very reduced in strength. Hugo White, in his history of the DCLI, puts the army's plight in plain language:

> 'Imaginative collective training barely existed, for this cost money. However, ceremonial drill was cheap and this, together with an orgy of spit and polish, occupied much of the soldiers' working day. This alone might have been demoralising if the Regiment had not thrown itself wholeheartedly into sport.'

George Millett was certainly a subaltern who made the most of those spare hours, taking active part in a variety of team and field sports. Then on 13 December 1930, George married Rita Maude

Bagster at Ticehurst in Kent. As they left the church, fellow officers provided a ceremonial guard of honour for the couple.

From 1931 to 1934 George had his first taste of army responsibility as Adjutant of 2 DCLI. This was a managerial role that was certainly a challenge to his stammer – especially when the battalion moved to Gibraltar in 1932. Rita went with him to Gibraltar and their first son, Andrew George, was born there in December 1933. While stationed there, Rita and George rode a great deal. They hunted in Spain and he played polo and rode in point-to-points. It was while the family were on home leave that George was told he was to be transferred to the regiment's first battalion and take a draft of men to fill the ranks during a posting to Razmak in the mountains of the North West Frontier – badlands of the Empire. He was not happy at leaving his family and especially cross about leaving the second battalion that had become his home.

But Rita and Andrew were able to join George in India in November 1935 as the battalion moved from Razmak to Dinapore, a well-established British cantonment on the Ganges in eastern India. All three returned on 'privilege leave' to Britain as my mother had contracted what was thought to be polio. Later George went back to India to take up the place he had earned at the Staff College in Quetta. At the end of that course the commandant wrote a report on my father. In it is the first written evidence I have found of his stammer:

A man with very high ideals and a high standard in life. Reliable in every way. He has great character & is a leader of men.
He has plenty of confidence and yet is charming & modest in his manner. He gets on well with everyone. A likeable personality.
His military knowledge is well above the average and he has done

> *well throughout the year. He has a good brain which he makes*
> *good use of.*
> *Tall, spare & fit. He is a keen horseman and shot. He has a slight*
> *impediment in his speech but he has not let that affect him.*
> *He will make an excellent staff officer well suited for employment*
> *with troops.*

That mention of a 'slight impediment in his speech', is not, to my mind, satisfactory evidence of the severity (or otherwise) of my father's stammer. I take it as a typically bland phrase used by writers of such reports. It reminds me of attempts to downplay my own stammer: so as a school poetry recital competition approached, I would be assured that I would be fine, '… after all you've only got a slight stammer' – they might even have used the 'impediment' word. Throughout his many letters my father never referred to his stammer. Occasionally he would mention he had not felt like making a speech, but that was never linked directly to his stammer. Neither of the other two confidential reports about him that have survived mention his stammer – or a speech impediment.

After George left India in December 1938, he began his course at Minley Manor Senior Staff College in the New Year. The course was interrupted by the outbreak of the Second World War. He was appointed a third grade General Staff Officer (GSO3) at 1st Corps' headquarters with the British Expeditionary Force. He left for France on 19 September 1939. During the war years that followed Dunkirk, my father held various Staff Officer posts and took his first command of a battalion – the DCLI's 4th battalion which was guarding part of the east coast and training men for the North Africa campaign. Then at the beginning of November 1942 he was picked to join the London headquarters of 1 Corps and began work on the planning for D-Day.

In June 1944 he landed in France with 1 Corps. He took command of the King's Shropshire Light Infantry's second battalion on 12 July 1944 and brought them through some bitter fighting, some heavy losses, many interesting places, meeting interesting people as well as many boring admin-filled days, to Holland. On the way he heard first-hand accounts of the terrors, tortures and killings committed by the German occupiers. In terribly wet and cold winter weather they settled on the banks of the River Maas – within rifle shot of Germany. There he was killed while on an early morning patrol. We will return to that day after we take a closer look at some important episodes in my father's army career – episodes that prove he was determined and successful in beating his stammer. They also prove his steadfast character and resilience.

12.

DUNKIRK

On 30 May 1940 – or thereabouts – George was evacuated safely and uninjured from Dunkirk. The terrifying events leading up to the chaotic evacuation from Dunkirk stand in stark contrast to the eight months of the 'phoney war', during which George Millett was with the British Expeditionary Force (BEF) in France – a Staff Officer with 1 Corps. It was rather like being on 'Les Grandes Manoeuvres' of old. There was training. There were defensive lines to be seen to. There was a lot of eating. There might be time for some recreational riding. There was time for entertainments with visiting stars and lesser lights from the music halls. There was time to hold a cocktail party for a recently engaged colleague and a dinner for alumni from the Senior Staff College. Postal communications with the home country were so good that George offered to send some French butter home to ration-hit Blighty. He even had two spells of home leave during those eight months – one over Christmas 1939. He was based in Douai. For a time he shared a billet in a French home with another staff officer, Captain Ken Exham. The 1 Corps HQ's office was in one of the town's closed infant schools. Although disappointed in his own ability with the French language, he was getting used to French life – and French breakfasts:

> Ken and I have our breakfast at a little café on the way to the office, it's easier than wasting time going to the mess & I have quite adopted the coffee + bread & butter idea.

When the evacuation began, he locked the school-cum-office and kept the key. Many months later, once he was back in France in 1944, he noted in a letter that Allied troops had just liberated Douai, and told his wife, Rita, that the key to the school was still on his key ring at home.

However 'phoney' the war was, George relished a 'North West Frontier fix' with a visit in February 1940 to the BEF's Indian Mule Corps:

> A very nice major in charge took us to see the mules – very small ones & perfectly sweet. All absolutely quiet. We 'waded' in donkeys all semaphoring their ears at us & nuzzling. I did enjoy it ... I talked some quite passable Urdu!

What happened to those mules, donkeys and their Indian minders during the chaotic retreat before the German advance, does not bear thinking about. Their role in supporting the BEF was never fulfilled – and had probably been rather poorly thought out. Much the same could be said of the BEF's defeat by the rampaging German tanks as they swept through Belgium and northern France. While I was growing up, the history of Dunkirk was, for me at any rate, a bit obscure and was certainly never properly explained. How could an army, let alone a country, be saved by those little boats? With continuing emphasis on the little boats, it was referred to as a 'miracle'. I do recall a sermon in the school chapel from a clergyman dressed in a red cassock with some medals on his chest. Perhaps it was an anniversary of the 'great evacuation'. With a booming, parade ground voice, he was comparing the feat of the little boats (he called them 'little ships') first to the Spanish Armada, on the grounds that the weather had been in our favour on both occasions, and secondly to the feeding of the five thousand. At which point the boy next to me whispered rather loudly: 'They'd need more than that bread and those fishes to feed that army.' I do not think that sermon helped me understand what Dunkirk was really all about.

I heard nothing about how and when my father had made it to safety. It was only when I read his letters home and tried – adding archive documents, memoirs and biographies – to piece together his part in those dreadful events, that I realised what an extraordinary and threatening time it had been. The evacuation and the days leading up to it, were truly chaotic – I found plenty of evidence for that.

At times of existential defeat, of loss and distress, you can tell a great deal about a person's resilience, professionalism, temperament and firmness of character. Equally, in such circumstances I am sure that any obvious lack of any of those elements would be quickly revealed. George Millett landed at Dover or Folkestone, exhausted and unable to speak, was put on a train and ended up near Tetbury in Gloucestershire.

Amidst the chaos, it is difficult to establish precisely when my father was evacuated. In some documents dates appear to be unreliable. Perhaps events taking place in the hours either side of midnight were simply attached to wrong dates. However, my father's first note to his wife after leaving Dunkirk is clearly dated 30 May 7.30 am:

'Dear Darling, Am in England. Destination and task at present unknown ... Love, Tigs'

Using that nickname (short for Tigger) he made sure Rita knew the note was genuine and he was safe. Next came a typed generic message – probably supplied by the Women's Voluntary Service: 'ARRIVED ENGLAND. LETTER FOLLOWING'. It is dated 31 May 1940 and was posted at Swindon – presumably when his train stopped for refreshments. It is signed 'George'. The following day Rita received a telegram: 'In England quite well love George.' There is no sender's address, but we can just read: 'Time handed in: 10.59', and it has the same date – 1 June – as his first full letter home, so perhaps it was sent from Tetbury in the hope it would reach Elstead before his letter:

I sent you various p.c.s & letters on our way in the train yesterday. Most annoying, we passed through Guildford [about ten miles from Elstead]. We only stopped a short time. The only people near had found husbands & things & I was just beginning to write a request for them to phone you when we went on. I could not ask as I was dumb! I have lost my voice & it was just at the worst patch – it's coming back now. I controlled a bridge & dealt with traffic mainly French from 9 p.m. to about 4 p.m. when I got relieved – so no wonder the vocal chords went a bit.

'Dealing with traffic' is his way of saying he spent nineteen hours yelling at pretty frightened and panicky drivers – many of them French. In fact, he was saving lives. Keeping the stream of trucks driven by French and British troops moving and dispersing them as they reached the outskirts of Dunkirk, he was preventing them becoming easy targets for German planes. We should note that having to shout over the noise of retreating trucks, though bad for his throat, was a good thing – most stammerers can be fluent when they shout!

George's letter to his wife continues:

I have lost everything except I think my sense of humour! However we have been fixed up with a razor etc & some clean clothes. I don't know what is happening yet, I must find out as I can be useful in sorting things out.

Don't listen to too much pessimism. We have come out of worse jams than this & if the French can pull their socks up as they seem to be doing, we shall stage a come back alright.

He continues – 'without being alarmist' – urging his wife to get someone to dig a slit trench in her garden and away from the house: 'Just a precaution – a narrow trench is the safest thing in the world.' This from a man who had witnessed German planes strafing troops as they waited on Dunkirk's beaches and along approaches to the town. The next day George had a telephone chat with his wife, Rita, and son, Andrew – then aged six and a half. George – and another 'evacuee' – had been taken in by the owner of Doughton House in Tetbury. He felt very at home there as his host had taught the princes polo and had a motto, my father wrote, 'drink hearty & often'. For all that, my father was keen to get back to work and reflected on his life with the BEF as a 'non-fighting' Staff Officer:

I've wired the War Office & bothered the local Brigadier, & so can do no more than sit back & get fat, though it tries one's patience a bit. However everyone has learned that [although] it is no fun being a non-fighting soldier, one got a full share of 'bloodiness'!

Rita was obviously very, very keen to go and see him in Tetbury. Luckily her pleas were answered when he was allowed some days home leave. This was especially welcome as she had been 'a bit ill' for several months – certainly ill enough to be treated by the local GP and to spend many weeks confined first to bed and then to the house.

Aged about ten or eleven, I remember an end of school term general knowledge test: 'Who knows the name of the town from which much of the British army was evacuated in 1940?' Hands shot up around the class. Mine did not. This was partly, of course, because Dunkirk's initial hard 'D' would have caught me out. It was also because I did not want anyone to ask me about Dunkirk. I knew my father had been there. I also knew the retreat had been a bit of a disgrace – rather like scoring an own goal on the football field. I did not want my father mixed up in a disgrace.

We must now spool forward to the King's Birthday Honours of June 1942. These included an OBE for my father.

Everyone here has been very kind and very sweet. Sergeants trot up & say excuse them but may they say they are so glad. The Mess are so pleased as they can now really work off a Cornish joke 'Oh be he O.B.E. bee ee' – or words to that effect – ad lib!

The only hint about the reason he was awarded his OBE comes in a letter to Rita about the announcement in *The Times*: 'It is rather fun and awfully kind of our "little man", I am sure it is his doing.' But which 'little man' was he referring to? I have made strenuous enquiries of experts at the National Archives and other archives, but have been unable to find any trace of the citation let alone the original recommendation. George had a habit of referring to all sorts of men he met or worked with a generic 'little man', so it is difficult to know whom he had in mind. However, I suspect this 'little man' was General Martel who was George's boss while he was with the 50th Division in 1940. They struck up a good relationship and Martel would certainly have heard all about George's exploits during the retreat to Dunkirk. My brother has a different theory. He thinks the award was made in recognition of George's work strengthening coastal defences and training troops for Hitler's planned invasion of Britain.

There is a pertinent story to tell about my father's OBE. When it came to decorations, the wheels turned slowly in wartime. It took from the June 1942 announcement until 9 May 1944 for him to receive his honour at Buckingham Palace with my mother and Andrew present – just a month before D-Day. This was the subject of one of very rare times my mother talked to me about my father, let alone about his stammer. It was a brief mention. She was chuckling at her memories of the day: 'As you can imagine, Daddy and the King did not get very far with the usual small talk.

They both stammered a lot and then there was a lot of silence. I think they both just smiled when it was time for Daddy to make his way back to his seat.' Andrew recalls that '... [Daddy] spent a long time with the King'. Perhaps it was nothing more than the King being intrigued to meet a senior officer who had successfully overcome his speech impediment. We're all in this stammering thing together. That's what they say ...

In Silver Jubilee Year 1977, I met the Queen aboard the Royal Yacht in Barbados and managed to say the right things without getting too stuck. Though I would have dearly liked to chat about the stammering silences between her father and my father at that investiture in 1944. I do wonder what her memories were of her father's stammer and the stress it so obviously caused him – and his family – once he became King.

13.

SOME PLAN!

FROM ESSEX TOWARDS D-DAY

On 23 April 1942 Temporary Lieutenant Colonel George Millett was appointed Commanding Officer of the fourth battalion of the Duke of Cornwall's Light Infantry – and had to leave the temporary family home in Salisbury for Essex. He had achieved his first command. He was in command of men – many of them from Cornwall – and he was involved in their well-being and their training. He was a happy, if very busy, soldier. 4 DCLI was a territorial battalion full of barely trained men and very young barely trained officers. It took conscripts from Infantry Training Centres and had to turn them into drafts of men ready for action – mainly to replace losses during the see-saw North Africa campaign.

One sentence in an early letter from Essex shows what having a command meant to George – even though he rounds it off with a typically self-effacing phrase:

It is funny signing my name these days as myself and not always 'for' someone else. Quite grown up!

Or, as his DCLI friend, Richard Burbury, put it, when you have a battalion to command, 'You are at least stud duck of your own puddle.' That is something I too have felt during my career – though in far lesser circumstances. Being able to make your own ideas and plans become real gives a totally different feel to everyday work. If his stammer was anything like mine, he would also have found that responsibility calmed his stammer. With authority to wield, you can become much more fluent – well, most of the time. Above all he was back among Cornishmen with fond memories of Truro's famous pub and hotel, The Red Lion:

> We had such fun at dinner tonight. I had announced that the [troop] carriers must have names ... I suggested Cornish names...The CO's special carrier [i.e. George's] was unanimously christened Red Lion, brackets Truro! I don't know if we shall be allowed place names ... I said if we had hills my vehicle would be Mount Misery.
>
> The Pioneer Platoon is 100% Cornish. The other day the Pioneer Sergeant was heard to remark about some Englishmen, I think, 'Us don't want ee along of we'.

His strong kinship with Cornwall also shows in a letter in August which makes a very rare mention, very carefully phrased, of German air attacks on British towns: 'Bodmin & Truro got a nudge the other day. Quite sharp ones I am afraid.' Rita would have known how worried her husband was about the fate of friends and acquaintances threatened by German planes bombing and strafing towns in his county. Attacks like those – known then as 'tip-and-run' attacks – were also made on east coast towns. Several were quite close to his HQ. But in reply to Rita's query he downplayed them: 'I have heard a vague bump every now and again.' Reassuring language, heavily euphemistic.

George faced three major problems that somewhat blighted his time as CO in Essex. First there was the lack of officer support. When he arrived, his second in command was Robin Goldsmith – who had been with the DCLI since 1927. They obviously developed a very good working relationship. Then, suddenly, Goldsmith was promoted to a senior staff role at the newly formed Airborne Division's HQ. In George's words to Rita, Robin had been 'snatched away'. No replacement arrived until 8 June.

Another problem interrupting his normal workload was an accident on the battalion's new assault course in which a Corporal was killed. This course was set up on George's instructions as a key part of his fitness and training regime: 'We got an N.C.O. killed this afternoon on training which doesn't add to the gaiety of nations.' He was Corporal Nicholas E Hosking and he is buried in Penzance. The aftermath of this accident was long drawn out and meant postponing some home leave until it was settled. I bet he wrote a wonderful, gentle letter to the man's parents – with lots of Cornish references.

The other major interference followed a terrible accident at Southern Command where he had previously been a senior staff officer. The rehearsal for a live ammunition demonstration planned to impress Churchill and General Marshall (then Chief of Staff of the US Army) was to take place at Imber on Salisbury Plain. It was to show the devastating effect fighter planes firing cannon and machine guns could have on enemy troop convoys. The inexperienced pilot of a Hurricane Bomber, a twenty-one-year-old Canadian, mistook a large group of military observers for the column of dummy soldiers which was his intended target. Twenty-seven were killed and seventy-one injured.

The pilot, Sergeant William JA McLachlan, was from No. 175 Squadron based in Dorset. The Squadron had only been formed six weeks earlier and been operational for ten days. The day after the accident, the RAF Court of Enquiry into the 'Imber incident' was told that Lt Col CG Millett had previously organised a similar – but successful – demonstration at Southern Command. So when the Court Martial took place of Wing Commander JD Ronald, the officer in charge on the day of this awful accident, George was summoned to Wiltshire to give evidence in his defence. His letters home give no indication he was worried about appearing at this court martial. Unfortunately, the records of the Court Martial have not survived. We do not know what evidence George gave to the Court – and he certainly did not commit any hint of his evidence to paper in his letters home, though we do know he had spoken to her at length on the telephone about it. Perhaps he had aired with her worries over his ability to address the court. All we do know is that Ronald was acquitted.

After the verdict, RAF officers present said they would fly George back to Essex. He was driven to Old Sarum airfield near Salisbury, making a stop at Southern Command HQ for some chatter and so he could telephone old friends there. He also met Wing Commander Ronald's barrister – who had questioned him in court:

The defending K.C. was a nice old man – he had offered to drive me back to London & was very sorry when he couldn't as he had to stay. He said he would have enjoyed it, I would have stayed at his flat & we would have got slightly drunk together – pity ... I told you how I rang everybody up. I would like to have seen them. A touching welcome from the telephone exchange.

That last remark sends a slight shiver down my spine: his stammer was a very recognisable call sign. This was, of course, many years before Subscriber Trunk Dialling. He and I had learnt how important it was to have good relations with the switchboard telephonists where you work. They can be very helpful indeed to a stammerer. There is a huge advantage if, before putting you through, a telephonist says 'I've Tony Millett of ITN in London for you Mr Dhillon'. There is then no need for you to try and say who and where you are – so making a stammerer's life a good deal easier.

After the RAF's own Court of Enquiry and the Court Martial, there was also an inquest at Warminster Town Hall on 26 June 1942. George was not called. The records of this inquest have also been destroyed. All we have is a report in the local newspaper, the *Warminster Journal*. The pilot blamed a haze that was lying across the downs and a cross-wind that 'must have taken him off course somewhat'. The coroner found that 'the 27 officers and men died from gunshot wounds sustained by misadventure while on military duty', adding:

'These mistakes are bound to arise in time of war, as all war is dangerous, and mistakes are made not only by pilots, but unfortunately probably by people in high command. I don't think we ought to feel that this young pilot is any different from hundreds of other pilots who do such good service for our country. He must feel very much anguished that his action resulted in so many casualties, but I hope he will continue to do good work for our country.'

The coroner's hopes were in vain. In those perilous times, no pilot was kept out of the sky for long and two days later Sgt McLachlan was back in the air with a 175 Squadron colleague. The two planes attacked enemy shipping off Cherbourg. They hit what they thought was a minesweeper of about 1,000 tons. It blew up. Then McLachlan was shot down and killed.

Early in September George was away from his battalion – a week divided between some home leave and meetings at the War Office about his new job in London. On 3 November he left 4 DCLI and became a senior staff officer with 1 Corps – part of the team planning the invasion of Europe. He had before him probably the most important eighteen months of his life: playing a significant role in the preparations for D-Day. He was working, at first, in Room 104, Norfolk House, St James Square and living, at least for a while, in the Royal Automobile Club. In the first letter he wrote to his wife from that new office address, written the day after their wedding anniversary, George took a moment to look back at their twelve years together:

I too much enjoyed our telephone conversation especially as it was the 13th. I do agree my darling we have had a very good twelve years, the last three a little interrupted but some very good patches in them. I am afraid you have had several misfortunes, but your grappling with them has been a source of considerable admiration to your friends & pride & example to me ... I agree our offspring appear adequate, people seem to like them. Yes, on the whole quite lucky we've been & very lucky I've been.

If not yet a date in the diary, D-Day was on the horizon. Among his many planning duties, the main one concerned training. He set out on a tour of Scotland to find suitable beaches for training exercises involving seaborne landings. He also did what he called 'Cobbett's tours' of training establishments across England and Wales. So it was not, at the start at least, all desk work. It even took him on a secret mission to Africa.

In June 1943 Rita Millett believed her husband was taking a break from his invasion planning to go shooting with friends in Scotland. Early for grouse, but there is always something to shoot even if it's only rock pigeons. In fact, unbeknownst to his wife, Lt Col Millett was on his way to the Mediterranean to observe Operation Husky and see at first-hand how landing craft fared in the mass seaborne invasion of enemy-held Sicily. They sailed from Liverpool on the troopship *Samaria* – a converted Cunard cruise liner which lacked hot water and was, much to George's regret, dry.

The mission had been initiated by COSSAC himself – Lieutenant-General Sir Frederick Morgan, Chief of Staff to the Supreme Allied Commander, otherwise known as D-Day's planner in chief. The group consisted of two Major-Generals, sixteen Lieutenant Colonels and a Major. On the journey, George spent time with Major Hon WM Berry, son of Viscount Camrose who was then a key figure in the British newspaper industry. After his war service, Berry became chairman of Amalgamated Press, chairman and editor-in-chief of the *Daily Telegraph* and deputy chairman of *London Weekend Television*. But my father spent most time with fellow Staff Officer, Lt Col JSB Lloyd, better known as Selwyn Lloyd – later a Conservative MP, Defence Secretary,

Foreign Secretary during the Suez Crisis and, later still, Speaker of the House of Commons.

Their mission was not a great success. A mix of inter-unit rivalries and fearful secrecy dogged the mission's every move. Why 'fearful'? The risk that the invasion of Sicily would involve major loss of life was very high. First George's mission was banned from leaving Algiers. Then they succeeded in getting that ruling lifted and went by a fleet of ancient cars to Tunis – where they were welcomed by General Alexander, whom George had known in BEF and Southern Command days. They were eventually flown to Malta – the invasion's naval base. There George received news that put the whole project in doubt. As he wrote in his mission diary:

'Got letter stating no one to cross to scene of operations. Had long indignation meeting and some gin. Seriously, as the mission is a complete flop we can only try to get home. It is maddening as I had a completely spare seat in a jeep & 30 Corps had laid everything on.'

Signed on behalf of General Alexander, then commanding the Eighth Army, this letter or memo or order, dated 10 July, was very fierce – threatening arrest for those ignoring it. George kept this vital document with his full response very safe – obviously preparing for any subsequent inquiry into the mission's 'lack of progress'.

My father did eventually land on a Sicily beach – briefly. And he did learn a lot about the way the various types of landing craft were being used – and about their shortcomings. On 15 July, he had got some members of the mission onto a tank landing ship (LST) going to Pachino beach – where Monty had landed four days before. The LST had a motto painted on its side: 'Ubique Pongos'. Apparently, 'pongos' were 'horny, attractive young army guys who will do anything to get with a girl for the night'. Even in the heat of war there was room for a ribald hint that life goes on.

I think it likely that Selwyn Lloyd was with George on this brief visit to Sicily as they later spent many hours together writing up notes from their trip. Their LST arrived off Pachino at about 7 am and went aground to discharge its cargo:

> 'About 14 ships lying off. Ducks [or DUKWS – amphibious trucks] working very well. Beach balloons up. Discharged ship's load in one hour. Went ashore for a few minutes!!'

Their departure from the beach area was delayed as another LST had gone ashore too fast and holed herself. Another lesson for the Overlord landings. And that was that.

My father had questioned innumerable staff officers and active service members of the invasion force. When push comes to shove you just have to approach people and trust they will not take fright (or worse) at your stammer – though a Lieutenant Colonel's crown and a pip would help! They had certainly learned enough to knit into a report. Sadly that report has not survived in the National Archives. My father's diary ends on a depressed note: 'So ends the story of the "Failure of a Mission".' During a protracted journey home he did get time to visit Carthage with Selwyn Lloyd – where they enjoyed a couple of swims in the sea.

Why am I bothering with this 'failed' mission? Well, for two reasons. First, it helps me get to know a little bit more about my father and the challenges he faced. The whole episode shows my father in a serious and, I believe, an admirable light. He was doggedly persistent in trying to fulfil the mission's aims. Secondly, it leaves me wondering what life might have been like if my father had survived the war – survived it with friends like those colleagues of his Selwyn Lloyd and Michael Berry.

Back in London, the planning work continued. The 1 Corps team were under enormous pressure. The stress of the final months leading up to D-Day was mounting and it was proving very wearing on those in the know. Once the planners had moved to Ashley Gardens near Westminster Cathedral, George was working again alongside Selwyn Lloyd. Much later, Lloyd explained to his biographer that the pressures on him were more intense at Ashley Gardens in the spring of 1944 than throughout the Suez Crisis. And writing in the 1 Corps HQ official 'war diary', my father did not mince his words: 'As was to be expected, work was intense and very long hours were worked by all the staff.' This took its toll:

'The prolonged planning and continuous long office work could not fail to have some adverse effect on the physical fitness of staffs. As the intensity of work continued up till the very end there was no opportunity for exercise or to get fit.'

Sometime towards the end of 1943, probably shortly before Christmas, the planners were overworked, tired and worrying endlessly about the complex issues facing them in the coming months. My father had known the date for D-Day since September 1943. That date was getting horribly close and there was still so much to do to ensure the plan was 'watertight'. As a boost to morale and provide a brief break from the solid slog of fitting together troops, units, ships, landing craft, generals, experts, tanks, Allied troops without enough English and so on, my father initiated an imaginative and cheerful exercise – just for the fun of it. Together they devised a military order dated 1 January 43 BC, detailing a new 'War Establishment' unit for the 'Heavenly Command' – a special 'Spiritual Aid Detachment'. It did, of course, have its own acronym: WE SAD. Undoubtedly an acronymic *double entendre*.

This make-believe unit was to be led by a Chief Priest aided by a Grade One Samaritan. The twenty-seven strong unit included twelve artisans, an acolyte, a shepherd, one 'whitener, sepulchre' and, at officer level, two 'Virgins, foolish (May be A.T.S.)' and two 'Virgins, wise (In short supply in hot climates)'. Attached to them was a 'Mobile Font Unit' complete with godmothers ordinary and godmothers fairy – and a sanitary man. The list of equipment needed was lengthy. Amongst the thirty-five categories were:

Two gross 'Pearls, castable' and one gross of 'Pearls, Grade 1'
Ten yards each 'Paths, straight' and 'Paths, narrow (Paths, primrose may be used in lieu')
22 'Panoplies'
22 'Haloes, nets, camouflage'
2 'Lamps, virgin, wise, full' and 2 'Lamps, virgin, foolish, empty'
7 'Vices, assorted'
200 'Harps, harping'
1 'Gates, pearly, left' and 1 'Gates, pearly, right'
1 set 'Walls, collapsible (Jericho pattern)'
5 'Fingers, moving, writing'
and 10,000 'Tracts, uplift'… and so on.

It was all a light-hearted, tongue-in-cheek take-off of the detail and language that wove its way through the orders they were drawing up every day – and long into every night. Then, of course, as usual some senior worrier had second thoughts:

Reference attached WE SAD type 'A', it is represented in an operation of this nature, where actual difficulties of replacement arise, that a full complement of 5 Virgins, foolish (i.e., the addition of three) is essential (these may be Warrant Officers) – if the above addition is accepted the corresponding increase in oil lamps virgin foolish will be necessary.

And so it went on – a squib. A parlour game with suggestions fired in thick and fast from assembled planners and clerks. Suggestions nearest to the bone were undoubtedly weeded out in case the final Order found its way to mothers, wives or sweethearts.

Back in the real world, staff officers had to cope with multiple changes in formations and their use, and also with the ever-increasing size of the force that was being trained and assembled. The strength of 1 Corps on 1 July 1943 was 523 officers and 9,950 other ranks. By 14 September 1943 those numbers had risen to 633 and 11,981. The need for a Beach Sub-Area HQ, Beach Groups, Beach Signals Sections, Ordnance Beach Detachments, Beach Recovery Detachments and then a whole extra follow-up infantry division to land on D-Day evening, all added thousands more men and as many complexities. On 6 June 1 Corps would land 50,000 men on its two beaches – Juno and Sword. Another 8,000 men of the Airborne Division (under 1 Corps control) would land at the very east of the invasion front. Churchill told the House of Commons on 6 June that commanders had reported everything was going to plan: 'Some plan! This vast operation is undoubtedly the most complicated and difficult that has ever taken place.'

George was not entirely happy with his lot. In his letters there are brief cries of frustration and expressions of his desire to return to commanding soldiers rather than pieces of paper. In October 1943 he wrote: 'Wish I could go back to 4 DCLI', and in April 1944 he mentioned friends he had left behind in Essex, adding: 'I liked my soldiers.'

When did Rita gather that her husband was going to war in mainland Europe? Did she take the hint when on 4 April 1944 George told her that he and his fellow Staff Officers had been issued with new headgear? Their caps would be highly unsuitable for everyday wear on or behind the front lines:

I wore my new Berry 'at this evening – after dark! Very dashing.
And he enclosed a pencil sketch of the new beret look. But he still could not tell his wife where he was based. 1 Corps HQ moved as D-Day neared and stress levels rose:

This address [HQ 1 Corps, Army PO, England] will always find me – that's what it's for. Of course it may change for that of a Salisbury loony bin, but I will let you know when the symptoms become acute!

In October 1943 he had forgotten his wife's birthday. In February 1944 he got his younger son's birthday wrong by three weeks. His mind was on other and vital matters – constantly. He had obviously had more than his fill of planning conferences at some of which he had to speak – another challenge for him. The plethora of conferences was on his mind as he took a break in St James's Park:

I went to commune with the ducks in the park but hadn't much time. Unfortunately they look so like a large conference. They wear very much the same expression & bob about just like members of a conference do mentally. However they are rather nice.

Despite his attempts to downplay his work load and lack of sleep, my father really did get overtired – as his letter of 8 February makes clear:

So sorry I missed writing yesterday. We have been busy and there wasn't a real opportunity. I have been ordered to 'go away', the Brigadier being 'Sick of the sight of me', so I am just writing this ... and then am going to bath & bed.

While still in London his nights had been badly disturbed by the Luftwaffe's so-called 'Baby Blitz' on London which lasted from January through to May 1944 - and to which my father referred in his usual oblique way: 'There was a noise in the night'. And later: 'I am having an early night tonight, so let's hope it is a quiet one.' There was another interrupted night on 19 February:

I had a good night on Friday. A lovely bath and early bed. Then I was woken up [by] the racket! I was cross. However I went to sleep before the all clear. Very angry I was.

His tiredness and stress increased as their plans started to be put into effect with the concentration of troops and equipment closer to the south coast – as the letter following his last visit home before D-Day explained: 'I am afraid I was rather dumb the first evening, but I was very tired which is why I was sent away – I had had about enough!'

Of course there were many other officers with different responsibilities within this vast planning network. There is in the National Archives one document, a single page, that tells us a great deal about the meticulous planning for the Allied invasion. It has nothing to do with my father's particular role. It is headed 'MOST SECRET'. Its subject is 'SEA SICKNESS REMEDIES'. It is dated the 12 March 1944 and is addressed to The Under Secretary of State at the War Office and is signed off for 'Major-General i/c Administration for 21 Army Group' – the British headquarters formation assigned attack Hitler's Europe from the west.

It begins prosaically enough:

'It is now possible to state the requirement of 21 Army Group of boiled sweets, biscuits and chewing gum for the alleviation of sea sickness.'

The quantities needed to try and keep soldiers from seasickness, standing upright and fighting fit after their sea crossing in those far from stable landing craft through unreliable seas, were simply enormous. Each man would need an ounce of boiled sweets, two ounces of biscuits and a pack of chewing gum. That meant the Under Secretary at the War Office would have to find: 6,250 pounds of boiled sweets, 12,500 pounds of biscuits and 100,000 packets of chewing gum.

But the document goes on to give the government an even greater challenge. There was going to be '... a full scale trial of the use of these items ... in exercises taking place not before 30 April.' That took the totals to 10,625 pounds of boiled sweets, 21,250 pounds of biscuits and 170,000 packets of chewing gum. It was a demand that made a significant hole in the nation's rations for the spring months of 1944.

As the exhausting month of May 1944 was drawing to a close, my father was sent away for a couple of days home leave. While the 1 Corps HQ staff were dispersed to their Marshalling Areas, George was at home in Elstead. It was, I was told by my mother, the occasion photos were taken on the sunny front porch of Quarter Acre in Ham Lane: my father in uniform, with his 1 Corps' badge of a white spear on a diamond background (in fact a red background), and myself with my blonde curls and a teddy bear called Ter. They show me on the ground looking up at my father and then sitting on his lap. I am not sure whether they are the saddest photographs or the most inspiring. They are the photographs I saw every day as I was growing up. They show the man I saw as my father. An image I can catch in my mind's eye at any moment of any day. It looks almost idyllic, but there have always been questions about that day: how had he reacted to my decidedly uneven, stammery speech? A question that can never be answered.

He was at home during the warm and sunny spell of Monday, 29 May till the afternoon of Wednesday, 31 May 1944. They drove to Aldro School to see Andrew. Then on Tuesday they parked me somewhere, and went off for an evening and night *à deux* at The Crown Inn in nearby Chiddingfold. With coffee, drinks and early tea on 31 May it cost £2.14.9p. That Wednesday evening, back in his Cobham office, he wrote to Rita to thank her for 'a very good spot of leave'. It was, he warned, to be a short letter '... as I've only seen you about four hours ago.' He was delighted with their 'holiday': 'I am so glad you were able to take a holiday even such a short one. I do hope it made a little change.' He continued:

I had a good run back. I filled the car with four very hot
(+) Wrens who had obviously been on a short pass and were
footing it in the middle of nowhere – my driver with the
nice smile was sufficient chaperone I felt. (+ hot = from
walking in the sun!)

That cheers me up. However worried about planning decisions
and with his stammer probably acting up due to his tiredness,
he was still happy to chat away – defying his stammer – with the
'very hot Wrens'! He adds one hint that he would very soon be
travelling again: 'Fraid letters will take a little time but will fetch
up eventually'.

14.

D-DAY AND NORMANDY

After two nights on board their transport ship, 1 Corps Headquarters went ashore on D-Day+1. We know very little about George's D-Day and the few days that followed – and can only imagine his anxiety that the plans they had sweated over were working properly. Before he got onto the beaches, he faced a tricky surprise. Either on D-Day itself or early on the day they went ashore, George was summoned from his ship to see Montgomery on his ship:

> I am not good at going to ships in a rough sea in small boats. I had to go and see Monty!!! And the sea took the boat away leaving me on a rope ladder like a monkey – most undignified! I did join the Army not Navy – unfair I call it ...
>
> The Army Commander talked to me while I was emptying the sea out of my boots & said he would move me when poss but I had been 'a great standby' where I was – nice of him!

His first proper letter home from France was written on 11 June and was brief and full of exclamation marks:

> I believe I am allowed to say that I am abroad but perhaps you guessed! I have known too much for too long hence my silences on leave! I have been 'in the know' since September!

However, he also had to record the D-Day deaths of two close friends from the regiment. It was nearly three weeks before he felt able to reveal to Rita a very, very brief view of D-Day:

> D-Day was a remarkable sight – all that enormous armada all assembled. It was also amazing having a completely quiet trip over. There was little bombing on the two nights I stayed on the ship, but v. few aircraft really.

It is also clear from his letters in June and early July that now they were fighting the enemy, George did not much enjoy his work on the Staff. He writes that he did not 'get out much' – his code for saying he was kept away from the fighting. In fact, of course, he was never very far from fighting. On 18 June he wrote and signed his last will and testament. It was witnessed by Guy Shacklock and Dick Bethell – both long-term Royal Artillery friends: 'Certified this was written on service and no stamp was available.' I was surprised – shocked even – to discover that once ashore in France, one of his staff officer duties was to hold press conferences for the party of journalists attached to 1 Corps. He told Rita that when he addressed the press corps he felt 'like Roosevelt' – the great proponent of chatty press conferences:

> [Newspapers] *are* bad – considering the time one spends (wastes) briefing war correspondents daily. It's not clever

... I was amused to see the results of a 'press conference' almost verbatim in the paper! I wish they would all do so they might not write such tripe at times!

It was a chore he could have done without: 'I am getting tired of playing my "gramophone record" to war correspondents. But I suppose the great British public require it.'

I do wonder how he got on in those press briefings. He held information vital to the journalists' work, he held the whip hand, so his stammer might not have been too much of a worry. As the military were in complete control of just about everything except the weather and the enemy's plans, he could certainly have put any annoying or rude journalists in their place. With my own experience of cantankerous hacks in mind, I wonder how those wartime hacks reacted to a stammering Lieutenant Colonel. I hope they were understanding and respectful. There is always one rotten apple who, during those press briefings, could make sly digs at my father's speech – behind his back or to his face. I know very well the feelings of disquiet, even uneasy fear, that would haunt his day.

His main task was drawing up and signing off operational plans for the continuing and troublesome task of capturing Caen. Then on 6 July, just before they were to make another attempt on Caen, the commanding officer of one of 1 Corps' infantry battalions, the Second King's Shropshire Light Infantry, Lt Col Jack Maurice, was killed by an enemy shell. In the words of that battalion's history: 'He had commanded the Battalion for two years and was dearly loved by all ranks. His death cast gloom over the battalion just as it was again to go into action.' With this officer's death George's world suddenly changed – utterly. Monty was as good as his word, and George was appointed as 2KSLI's commanding officer. He took over command at 1600 hrs on 12 July. It happened to be a day for rest and maintenance of equipment. The battalion's war diary reported: 'Apart from occasional enemy aircraft flying over during the night, we were undisturbed.'

George was very open when he wrote to his wife about the task he had been given:

> I have been here 24hrs now & still feel a little lost. But that was natural. Everyone is most charming and all said they were pleased to see me though most had never seen me before! ... The previous CO, who I knew well, was very much the ideal of the regiment and every single person adored him. It's a lot to live up to. However it is great being out again with men. They have just had a most successful battle and are having a rest ... I have today signed my name as myself and not 'for' anyone else – tremendous sensation.

He was marking the same sensation he had felt when he took over his first command in April 1942. I will never know how he went about taking over from such a revered commanding officer. He certainly had a lot of talking and reassuring ahead of him.

What was this new battalion? The first years of 2KSLI's war were spent on guard duties in the West Indies. They were called home in February 1942 and joined 4 DCLI and 5 DCLI in 136 Brigade in Essex. So George had got to know Maurice and many 2KSLI officers – as they were brought up to strength to be a fighting battalion. They were then transferred to 185 Brigade, part of the 3rd Infantry Division – also known as 'Monty's Ironsides'

– within 1 Corps. On D-Day they came ashore on Sword Beach.

In George's letters home there is, understandably, a great deal of reassurance for Rita: 'I am v. well & getting sufficient sleep, so all OK' and 'I am being awfully good & cautious my love ...' He explains to her that as CO he has

> ... three complete characters in my entourage. – Jones the carrier driver, Cooper batman and Arnell orderly or body guard. They combine in seeing I have food & tea & so on & I am never allowed to go about alone!

In August he reports how the Brigade commander came over the radio to tell George to halt his battalion's advance immediately and move no further forward, adding to his radio operator '... remind him he has a wife and children!'

Soon after he became 2KSLI's commanding officer, the battalion took part in another assault towards Caen. Days after working on the planning for this operation, with his new 'hat' George had to lead his battalion in this major battle. Suffice it to say it was successful, though it cost the lives of thirteen members of his battalion. This operation was covered in George's letters home in six words: 'We've been popping about a bit.'

We should pause briefly to consider my father's stammer a little further. Captain John Eaves had joined 2KSLI in September 1943 as their Intelligence Officer (IO). A very tall, fairly thickset man, he had been a solicitor before he was called up. A thoughtful and deliberate man, I was delighted to get to know him very well – though sadly only towards the end of his life. When I asked

John about his CO's speech he said it never occurred to him that it mattered and he emphasised how well my father communicated with the all the Battalion's soldiers: 'He loved chatting away to the men and loved joking with his officers!' John chuckled at the memory. The other veteran whom I go to know well was my father's signaller and wireless operator, George Bunting. He was a truly wonderful man. He was short, spare with twinkly eyes and a great line in light-hearted remarks – a trait that would have endeared him to my father. In 1944 he was 26. In civvy life he had been a GPO telephone engineer and in his spare time a runner competing in long-distance races for substantial prizes. So he was very fit and, despite his heavy load of radio gear, could easily keep up with my father – often just a couple of connecting cables' length away. George smiled broadly when I asked him about his commanding officer's stammer. He said that of course he'd noticed it though it didn't really get in the way. 'But,' he added with shrug of the shoulders, 'there were occasions when he was talking on my radio to HQ and he'd get a bit stuck – then he'd shout the words. And I had my earphones on!'

Sadly, both these 2KSLI veterans died too soon after I first met them.

The battalion's next engagement concerned a hill – or as the army prefers, a 'point'. It was held stubbornly by a number of German units and was sorely needed for artillery observation posts so rear gunners could blast away at the enemy forces blocking an essential and urgent further move eastwards by British and American forces. Their target was Falaise where Germany's resistance in Normandy would eventually fall apart. This hill was Point 312. John Eaves, who as Intelligence Officer had been very close to the planning for this assault, assured me Hill 312 had been flagged as 'a hill of great strategic importance'. He was very proud of the part he had played in the battle and wanted to take his wife to see where it had been fought. But he could not find it on any modern French map. Being a determined fellow, he wrote (in his perfect French) to France's mapping authority and they replied with a full explanation for its disappearance. After the war many heights had been reassessed and 312 had been demoted to 309. And there it was on the map – some miles south-east of Vire and some yards north-west of Les Sources, among farming land and hedgerows between roads D512 and the D524.

Alison and I have been to see Hill 309. It looks quite misleading from the foot of a large field. It just seems like a long and gentle slope between high hedges. In fact, when you get to the top you see very clearly why it was such an important feature – from the escarpment you get a clear view to Tinchebray and miles beyond. In the battalion War Diary, which was always the responsibility of the CO, my father called Point 312 '... the dominating feature between Vire and Tinchebray'. It seems my father dictated the diary, perhaps over the radio, as an orderly had typed every reference to the hill as '.312', thinking 'point' meant 'decimal point'. Eventually each mention of the 'decimal point hill' had to be corrected in ink by the CO!

Preparations and recces for this operation got off to a bad start on 6 August when they were caught by German troops and had to abandon their jeeps until after dark: '... while the CO and W Company Commander crept ignominiously through the ditches back up the slope to Brigade HQ'. The early advance was slow and painful. 3 Division's Intelligence Summary up to midnight on 9 August took a broader view of this hill:

> 'The battle for Pt. 312 is inclined tonight to be overshadowed in interest by the battle for France. But the first is our concern so let us consider it first.'

Perhaps this report was written by a soldier who in civilian life had been a history teacher with broader views of events and awareness of their relative importance. The Division's Intelligence Officer concludes:

> 'So the question arises whether the enemy with whom we have today been in contact will fight or run. The answer is more likely to be found in the general rather than the local enemy situation.'

After a bit of a 'scramble' to get away at 0900 hrs on 11 August, the Operation began with good news for the men of 2KSLI: the first village on their route to Hill 312 was undefended. But they still took casualties along the way. Then, having been told by the CO to take a nearby hill – Pt. 272 – they were held up: 'The enemy, in small machine-gun parties, were roaming about in copses and gardens and lanes, firing bursts at close range then nipping away.' 2KSLI's W Company reached the top of Pt. 272: 'We contacted Major Brooke-Smith of Y Company, and decided that further warfare could wait until we had brewed some tea.'

From the operational logs of the Corps, Division and Brigade HQs, it is obvious that capturing this important vantage point was an extremely difficult and strenuous struggle. Only at 0850 hrs next morning did 3 Division confirm: 'KSLI finally on Pt. 312'. The order came from Division to Brigade to make Pt. 312

'firm', but to allow for 'observation posts to be established for the artillery'.

The 3 Division Intelligence Summary explains the problems the battalion had faced:

'It was chiefly the difficulty of the country which made the going so slow - though the enemy had mined most road junctions, cross roads and used other delaying devices. The enemy also took full advantage of the many hedges and in places it was necessary to make small but deliberate deployment to capture each field.'

Normandy's infamous *bocage* country – with its tall hedgerows and sunken lanes and small fields – had taken its toll. Finally, George could report in the War Diary:

'Soon we had five artillery Observation Posts amongst us, including one from both sides of the flanking American and British Divisions. Pt. 312 had a magnificent view of the countryside and Lt General   O'Connor,   commanding   8 Corps, visited the feature to make a recce on 13 August.'

There is, understandably, no evidence in his letters written on those August days of this battle or its losses or its amazing success. 2KSLI gave British and American forces the chance to liberate more towns – such as Flers – and chase the German forces into the 'Falaise Pocket', from which few escaped. John Eaves told me – and he was most emphatic about this – that in his opinion the successful capture of Hill 312 by 2KSLI was my father's most significant achievement as the battalion's CO. John Eaves had been there, he had read all the books about the Normandy campaign and he was cross – cross that Hill 312 only featured in specialist histories of the units involved and was ignored in campaign histories. Sadly, John was not well enough to visit Hill 312. He died in June 2007.

It was only towards the end of the month that George told Rita something about the battalion's success in taking Point 312 – and even then he did not give the Hill (or Point) a number – just in case some 'unfriendly' person read his letter as it made its way to Elstead:

> We captured a hill which appeared in the papers some weeks ago – it wasn't all that strongly held! Everyone was very excited about this & came to see it, so the Brigadier brought me a lovely board saying:
>
> Point ----
> Admission 10 francs, apply
> to OC 2KSLI.
> You want the best views
> we have them.
>
> I duly stuck it up & it's there now as far as I know. I had to let the Corps Commander [O'Connor] off his 10 francs! I said he could be an honorary member.

That is a signboard I would love to have. In his diary, 3 Division's Major-General Whistler called 312 'a monster hill' and said its capture had allowed the Division to liberate Flers – 'a considerable town smashed up completely'. 2KSLI were fortunate to skirt round Falaise. A Major sent to count abandoned equipment and the German dead, described Falaise as '... the most devastated town yet seen, a holocaust of dead German horses and horsedrawn transport.' The men's only relief from their loathsome tasks was, he wrote, 'gallons of cider' and 'pints of calvados'.

At Tinchebray on 18 August, 2KSLI began a spell of maintenance and reorganisation. With reinforcements arriving daily, by the end of the month the Brigade was 'over strength' and rested. Part of the necessary reorganisation fell on George's shoulders:

> I have had a bloody day (far too bad to make it b-----y). I have had to sack my 2nd in command. He is a regimental figure having been in it 17 years. I am new. But I can't have blokes that 'soft pedal' and find difficulties instead of finding the answer to things. However it won't make things any easier as this battalion is so very regular. However it's right.

Major Wilson left on 20 August. Perhaps timed to soften this blow to battalion stalwarts and steady morale, George had arranged for three sergeants to receive 'field commissions' – promoted to be officers. His bloody awful day must have involved a great deal of persuasive talk to his other officers – and when you feel on the back foot, the stammer can take advantage, adding to your problems.

On 3 September the brigade began two weeks of training and rest just north of the Seine at Villers-en-Vexin. It lies near the ruins of Richard the Lionheart's great Castle Gaillard, standing on cliffs above Les Andelys and the Seine: 'Battalion engaged in training mainly for operations in open country, wood clearing and river crossing.' Where would they need those skills?

Despite the training, it was quite a relaxing time. Some of the battalion 'even washed and went to Paris'. They were all able to eat inordinate amounts of fresh eggs and mushrooms – and they 'danced and sang'. Among the hospitable citizens of Villers-en-Vexin George met a Frenchman – with perfect English, but a cleft palate – who had been a volunteer link-man for ...

> ... 'the underground' & had passed through 100 baled out airmen. He had hidden some of them in his house for three months. Such cold courage is almost unbelievable. There is a woman in the village who was told that her two sons who were prisoners would be released if she gave away the organisation. She didn't. That's real courage. I seem to have changed my views about the French don't I! However there are good and bad everywhere, and it's very encouraging meeting the good.

His opinion of the French army had been soured by the rout of 1940. Now he invited 'the underground' volunteer to talk to some of the battalion:

> His sister-in-law & also a friend of the village priest had, however, arrived from two separate places in central France which had been occupied by the Boche with such dreadful stories of atrocities that he passed them on to the troops. Fulfilled my purpose even more. The stories are awful, really bad. We must get on the move again soon and kill some more Boche.

I find the contrast between this quite early knowledge of Nazi atrocities – here in unspecified detail – in rural France and the joy troops found among the liberated French to be almost breathtaking. Contrast those stories of the cruellest kind of atrocity with the story George heard from his new second in command, Guy Thornycroft – and passed on to his wife:

> He has just returned from a reconnaissance (we had to have some mushrooms). He went thro' the village that was so kind to one of the companies. Two bright young things rushed down the village street, stopped the jeep and said are you bringing the soldiers back, you must bring them back. We do want a dance & the mayor won't let us have one unless there are English soldiers.

Getting back to some sort of normality was fraught with minor problems!

During the Normandy campaign, John Eaves was a great help to my father as he spoke excellent French – essential for persuading people to billet soldiers and in finding fresh food. After their weeks of training with new recruits, the battalion held an all-ranks dance to thank the people of Villers-en-Vexin for their friendship and their hospitality. Invitations to the locals were arranged by the Mayor's daughter and my father was surprised she had persuaded so many of the nobility and gentry to attend – 'the impressives', as he referred to them. Before the dance ended, the CO felt he needed to say some special 'thank yous' – with the help of Intelligence Officer John Eaves:

> I made a speech at the end thanking the locals for their kindnesses etc etc. I said it in English for the troops and the impressives (!) and it was translated sentence by sentence into French by my I.O. He did it very well, especially as we only rehearsed it ten minutes before we gave it. The interpretation of speeches hasn't been done before and the 'Brothers Bimbo act' went over big!

I expect this speech to 'the troops and the impressives' proceeded pretty fluently – helped by a glass or two of local wine. But he had not flinched from making the speech.

15.

HOLLAND –

WET AND COLD AND MUDDY

The Normandy campaign had left 8,000 young men of Monty's Ironside Division as casualties – wounded and killed. We find the Division's Commander, Major-General Whistler, still in France and looking ahead a little anxiously to the next phase of their war on Hitler's Nazis – but, like my father, keen, after all their recent training, to see action:

'No doubt we will have some foul job to do fairly soon ... The Battalions are in very fine order indeed. I have never seen better men anywhere. Well seasoned, strong looking and very determined.'

That 'job' would indeed be 'foul'. It sent my father and his battalion into Holland – for the wettest, muddiest and coldest autumn and winter months of their lives. On 24 September my father wrote home:

I do not like the country we are in now & the weather is unspeakable.

The Battalion history agrees:

> 'It was one of the most depressing places in which we were
> ever to be situated. The weather was vile, pouring rain, the
> country low and waterlogged, the roads and tracks covered
> with mud and the ditches full of the decaying bodies of the
> enemy dead.'

On 11 November 1944, George's good friend Pat Daly of the
DCLI, who was now their Brigade's senior staff officer, let fly:

> 'Holland is hell. In Holland it rains and rains and rains.
> Today it snowed, yesterday there was a gale, and always
> it rains. In Holland there is mud: the fields are muddy,
> the roads are muddy, the streets are muddy, and always it
> rains. In Holland the people are plain, their faces are plain,
> their dresses are plain, their towns are plain, their houses
> are plain, and always it rains. In Holland there are no pubs,
> there are no cinemas, there are no parks, and always it rains.
> In Holland everyone goes to Church, in the afternoon they
> go to Church, in the evening they go to Church, always
> they go to Church, and always it rains. In Holland there
> is no laughter, no amusement, no life, and only funerals,
> always there are funerals, and always it rains. I do not like
> Holland. Holland is hell.'

A few days later my father had second thoughts on the wisdom of
sending Pat Daly's squib back to Surrey:

> I don't think I should publish Pat Daly's effort – although
> it is well worth it. I feel somehow the owners of the
> country, who treat it & themselves very seriously (we treat

it seriously, but not in the same way) might feel aggrieved.

I circulated it to companies to cheer them up.

The rain proved an ever-present frustration. Early in December, George posted his Christmas mail. To his brother's family he sent a post card showing a Dutch windmill and canal. Below the formal greetings he wrote one message the censor would pass: 'They've left out the rain in this picture'.

When not the Brigade's forward battalion, 2KSLI's companies were housed in farm buildings, cellars or were billeted in rooms within homes. The division's job was first to protect the routes through to Arnhem and then, when the Arnhem operation failed, to keep the Germans from counter-attacking across the River Maas. They were in an area of low-lying, marshy country west of the Maas called The Peel. The Dutch claimed that across the centuries none of their many invaders had succeeded in advancing across The Peel – in summer or winter. Indeed an American armoured division took a terrible mauling in the area. With dozens of armoured vehicles abandoned to the mud, they had to be withdrawn.

After the difficult capture of the town of Overloon and many small villages nearby, the biggest prize in The Peel was the town of Venray. Its population of 17,000 was swollen with some 8,000 refugees. The fifteenth-century church of St Petrus Banden was the pride of Venray – its iconic tower known as 'The Pearl of the Peel'. The Germans had put an observation post in the tower, reporting British positions to its artillery and rocket launchers. On 14 October thirty-six Allied Typhoon warplanes fired 284 60-pound rockets over Venray and British artillery targeted the church. It was destroyed – only the tower remained. That evening a huge fire raged in Venray – most of the town centre was in ruins. Two issues complicated the battle for the town: the Allied troops had first to cross the Moleen Beek – a wide and brim-full stream. Then inside the town there were the patients of two psychiatric hospitals – both were religious foundations, one for men, one for women. After two days of fighting they had to be evacuated. Days later the whole population of the town was evacuated. The main attack by 8 Corps came on 16 October. It was an appallingly nasty and bloody few days. Some of the fighting was at very close quarters as the Germans clung on street by street. 2KSLI's Intelligence Officer, John Eaves was badly wounded in the stomach, and, once back in England, spent many months in hospital. He told me the wound became a permanent problem and troubled him for the rest of his life.

This battle gave rise to the only wartime reference I have found to my father's stammer. In his account of 2KSLI's W Company during the battle for Venray, Captain Ryland wrote about the moments after they had crossed the Moleen Beek and were still on the outskirts of Venray:

'Our "O" Group was immediately mortared most accurately and at very close range. There were a lot of casualties. I have a confused memory of chicken coops leaping into the air scattering dead and live fowls in a flurry of feathers: of the disintegration of a man standing next to me: of the CO continuously and quite composedly stuttering into an 18 [radio] set: of lumps of steel appearing in Private Bennion's helmet and my haversack: of an attempt to take cover behind a disembowelled pig.'

This was war at its most terrible. At times it mirrored First World War conditions with the rain, the shelling, the rain, the mud, the endless rain and the cold. Captain Ryland's recognition of my father's stammer – or stutter – is absolutely straight. I take great solace in his word 'composedly'.

I have lived most of my life in total ignorance of my father's role in the fighting after D-Day – especially during those awful months in Holland. It was only when I got to grips with his letters and researched the battalion's role and met some veterans of the fighting that I got even an inkling of what he had been through. My friend George Bunting knew from his own everyday experience how near his Commanding Officer kept to the action. After all, his job was to carry the CO's radio set and keep it as close to my father as possible – and keep it working. George told me that my father was the bravest man he had known. Quite besides the occasional difficulty with his speech, I cannot begin to fathom how my father did it. I accept he was a professional soldier and well trained in how this type of warfare was fought. Even so, I have to admit that his kind of bravery is alien to me, quite beyond me. I find it totally admirable, but, I must also admit, totally incomprehensible. Hearing and reading about this battle, I find it impossible to realise that, besides the terrifying decisions he had to make and the confidence he had to show his troops, all the while he faced the perpetual challenge of his speech.

Venray was not a good place to be. The *Daily Telegraph's* reporter wrote (20 October): 'Overloon and Venray are wrecked as I have not seen villages wrecked since the long-drawn out battles around Caen and Falaise.' This article was mentioned in one of my father's letters home: 'I see the Telegraph had a lot of nice things to say about us.' There was still an embargo on mentioning individual divisions, brigades and battalions. All the news was merely in the name of the British Second Army.

In November and into the early days of December, things settled down a little. They watched V2 rockets launched by the nearby German forces against Antwerp and Britain. On 2 December there was a most unwelcome intruder as the War Diary reports:

'1900hrs a V2 dropped into the area of Z Company without causing any casualties to personnel. Considerable damage was caused by blast to houses within the area of some 400 square yards.'

Merely a misfired rocket – but a blunt and worrying reminder of what so many families in Britain had been facing.

The battalion was alternating between being 'in the line' and 'in reserve'. Entertainment was difficult to provide. The mobile bath unit was generally only available once a week. In the battalion history, Radcliffe made clear the general reaction to the flat, war-ravaged, waterlogged countryside beside the Maas: 'Not one of us will ever want to visit that area again even if offered a large bribe.' In these conditions keeping morale above water level was a full-time chore. My father must have done a great deal of talking to his troops.

The battalion's move back to the River Maas came on 16 December. The sudden order to move annoyed my father as he had lined up all sorts of social events: 'Pity. I had got 40 young women lent me by the next door C.O.!! Only for an organised dance.' Their new area was along the banks of the Maas between Broekhuizen in the north and Lottum in the south – a distance of about two kilometres. The forward companies were separated by thick woods that were probably mined and had unswept tracks. 'A policy of vigorous patrolling on our bank was started.' At the start of the month, Brigade HQ had warned the battalion that a German patrol had crossed the Maas near their new area. If it had got over the river, it had disappeared.

During the evening of Tuesday, 19 December, 8 Corps' War Diary recorded that Allied artillery fire had been brought down on an island in the Maas where preparations had been spotted for an attempt by German forces to cross the river. Some hours later a German patrol of about seven men was seen crossing the river: 'Fire was exchanged and they were not seen again, although the area was searched by 2KSLI.' The 3 Division War Diary for 19 December recorded: 'Enemy patrolling across river more pronounced.' It was a busy day along the river near Broekhuizen. 2KSLI's War Diary:

'10 V2's were reported to have been launched some 15 miles in front of left forward company. Some slight increase in enemy mortar activity without causing any damage.

2100 1st Bn Norfolks reported that enemy party of strength of 6 to 8 men had landed on their front.'

That evening, between calls and messages to my father reporting this activity, he was writing another letter home to Rita. This time he did have some news – pretty darn good news at that. Though it was tinged with a little disappointment. Lots had been drawn for the order in which the brigade's three battalion commanders would get home leave:

All being well, I look like getting leave on 29 January

... A most miserable man in my own regiment drew the three C.O.s and drew me last. I've told him he will never darken my doors again!! Anyway it's quite good.

Apart from that good news, he was looking to the future, discussing which school Andrew (known as Pip) should go to next. George was also commiserating with Rita about how cold the house in Elstead was. And complaining about his nights in Holland: 'cold, raw, wet, very cold, beastly, b-y & always it rains'. He hoped my imagination had calmed down a bit and said Rita should ask me if I was being good. And then he signed off:

Much love to Pip & A.J. & and all to you precious – loves you so very much. Always all your very own,

Tigs

Bless you.

C.G.Millett

That letter, with the promise of home leave, was the last letter my mother received from her husband.

We read a great deal about the figurative 'fog of war'. 20 December broke with real fog shrouding the River Maas. The 2KSLI War Diary recorded: 'Fog hampered visibility ...' and very early that morning:

'0110 Reserve Company (Z) reported the sound of two explosions to their front at a distance of some 500 yards. Shouting was heard and the words 'Stretcher bearer' ... were distinguished.'

It was decided the battalion would send out a recce patrol in the morning to check what the shouting and explosions had been about. It was assumed that during the night some Germans had crossed the river and walked into their own minefield. At 08.30 the CO and his bodyguard, Private Arnell, with a Sergeant from the Battalion's Pioneer Platoon and a guide from Z Company, led a patrol 'to recce the area of last night's incidents'. The War Diary carried this brief account:

'20 December – 0915 Explosions heard and report received that the Commanding Officer, Lt Col. C.G. Millett, OBE, his bodyguard and two other ranks had been killed in a minefield. The party had approached the body of a dead German and were examining the corpse when the explosion occurred.'

The battalion history has this version of events – written by Guy Radcliffe who had been my father's adjutant since the battalion entered Holland:

'When they arrived at the edge of the minefield the body of a German soldier was to be seen near two of our derelict tanks which had gone up on the mines. The Pioneers swept and taped a track up to the body, finding several mines, which were removed. What exactly happened will never be known, but it seems likely that the 'schmeiser' in the hand of the dead German had been booby-trapped and that whilst removing the weapon preparatory to obtaining identification of the enemy's regiment, one of the party also stepped on a mine. The explosion killed the Commanding Officer, his bodyguard, Private Arnell, and the Pioneer NCO, Sergeant Peever. The only other men who were near were all wounded.'

It is strange that Radcliffe only mentions three deaths. Strange too that they are not the same three names in the account sent to Peever's wife and recently published on a Second World War history website. This seems to be a diary entry sent as a letter by one of the Sergeant's friends. Its version of the events claims that the CO ordered Peever to take the machine gun off the German body: 'The dead man was heavily mined and the machine gun was the trap.' The writer calls the order 'foolish' – an understandable reaction when your friend has just been killed.

This desperate story continues with testimony in the letters of condolence my mother received in the following weeks. Most important is the letter from Captain Radcliffe written on 21 December. He prefaces his account as gently as he can: 'You will only have had one of those horrible official messages. I think that you would like to hear how he was killed ...':

'... Quite how we shall never know, but a mine went off and your husband and the other three men who were near were all killed instantaneously. The only other three who were anywhere near were wounded – none of them very gravely. I am afraid the only consolation in this tragic story is that he was killed outright, of that the Doctor has no doubt.'

Major John Sale was based nearby and confirmed that last point: 'All I can say is that he never suffered for one single instant. I reached him a few seconds after it happened.'

Later that day facts were hard to come by: at 10.20 on 20 December, 3 Division HQ received this message from 185 Brigade:

'CO 2KSLI and 7 or 8 [sic] men killed whilst clearing

minefield in their area. Could we have a section of Royal Engineers with mine detectors as soon as possible.'

185 Brigade's War Diary carried a single entry for 20 December. It confirmed the belief that it was a booby trap:

'... Investigation in the light disclosed that an enemy patrol had stumbled into an old enemy minefield. One dead German was found whose body had been booby-trapped. The booby-trap was not noticed and when the body was moved a mine exploded killing Lt Col C.G. Millett, OBE, Commander 2KSLI and killing and wounding several other ranks.'

One more version of those dreadful events will suffice. RSM Allen was a long-serving member of the KSLI. He had been in the regiment with Jack Lamb who, since he retired, was the licensee of the pub at the end of Ham Lane in Elstead. In January 1945 Allen wrote a lengthy letter to Mr Lamb who lent it to my mother and she copied out most of it. Having written of my father's '... fearlessness, untiring energy, his willingness to help anyone in trouble, he carved a groove for himself in the hearts of all ranks of the Battalion', RSM Allen recounts the events of 20 December as the patrol set out:

'Being a very conscientious type of man, he was with the leaders who were conducting the sweep. Suddenly a loud explosion was heard. Four men including the C.O. and his bodyguard lost their lives. While two more were wounded. It is presumed that one of the party stepped off the path which had been swept and detonated two or three mines. It was a great blow to the battalion.'

Those killed with my father were Private Sidney Lewis Arnell (aged 25 – my father's bodyguard and orderly), Sergeant William Leslie Peever (aged 27 of the Pioneer Platoon) and Corporal Charles Edward Gwatkin (aged 24). All four were buried at the Venray Cemetery on 21 December – with full military honours.

I have to accept that, despite my lengthy research efforts, we shall never know exactly what happened that morning beside the River Maas. It probably was a booby trap. It may just as easily have been that one member of the patrol did step off the path that had been cleared of mines. It could have been that one of the men slipped in the Dutch mud and set off a mine – or set off the booby trap. It hardly matters now.

Some of my father's character traits that I had only viewed from afar and were, of course, absent from his letters home, suddenly burst into the open with the astonishing array of letters to my mother from members of the battalion – and from older friends and previous colleagues and, of course, relatives. These were far, far away from the sadly formulaic, impersonal words of praise for those killed in action, words Siegfried Sassoon called in his poem *The Hero* the 'gallant lies' told to a mother 'that would nourish all her days'. These letters were very personal, many from front line colleagues.

On 31 December, Major John Sale was appointed second-in-command of the battalion:

'We had all served with him for some months past and had grown to like him as a man and admire him as a soldier. Under the most trying conditions he remained so cheerful and so unperturbed that our worries seemed to disappear. For his personal safety during battle he had little regard and was an inspiration to all of us.'

It was a theme Guy Radcliffe seconded:

'I cannot even begin to tell you how much the battalion will miss him. He was a great leader, always so calm, so unmoved by all that might happen. All the officers and men had the greatest respect for him.'

There was a letter too from the new Officer Commanding 185 Brigade, Brig EHG Grant. It is one of the most telling of all these letters – certainly not a letter composed for him by a staff officer:

'As you probably know, I only took over this Brigade within the last fortnight; but in the few days that I knew George I had not only formed a very high opinion of him but realised that I could rely on him utterly and completely. His shrewd sense of humour, which was such a delight, broke the ice of many of my earlier meetings and conferences and I cannot tell you how grateful I was to him for his thoughtfulness. To a stranger like myself the atmosphere of respect and love in which he was held by his battalion was extremely marked, and I know that his memory will remain very fresh with them.'

That man was my father – he really was. Like me, he had a stammer. I was too young to remember him.

My father's successor as CO of 2KSLI was Pat Daly – also of the DCLI. When George took over 2KSLI, he had been glad to find Daly's friendly face at Brigade HQ. As my father had explained to Rita, they had indulged in '... a little backchat over the ether every now and then!! I am afraid we make the troops giggle a bit.' Daly wrote to my mother:

'... I would like you to know that we all looked on George as one of the nicest and most kind hearted people that you could meet. He never said a hard word to anyone, and was always so kind and patient with everyone ... I know to my advantage how co-operative and understanding he always was. We were all delighted when we heard he was coming to us – so many of us knew him. It has all made his loss so much a personal affair for us all.'

Another long-standing friend and DCLI colleague was Hugh Bellamy – then CO of another of 185 Brigade's battalions, the 1 Norfolks. When Bellamy wrote to my mother he was in Sussex on home leave, but before he had left Holland he had seen the grave – 'neat and tidy and well cared for':

'Rita, he was a great man with all the highest qualities a man can hope to have. Brave, loyal, kindly, and with a sense of humour born of a happy heart. In all the years I knew him he was a wise counsellor and a friend to me, as indeed to many others. But I valued his words most during this campaign and if ever in any doubt I always went to his HQ and came away the better for it ... I can assure you the Army and this country have lost a great and good man whose qualities would be hard to attain.'

The battalion's padre, Rev FO Saunders, had only been with the battalion a couple of months, but he had spotted my father's ability to talk to the 'other ranks':

'He loved to get about among his men and they knew that he shared their discomforts and dangers. It was under such circumstances that he got killed. We were all very proud of him.'

My father's one-time second in command, Major Guy Thornycroft, emphasised George's 'cheerful disposition and thoughtfulness':

'It was not an easy task for him to take over a strange battalion, especially one that had been together for so long, but it was no time before he had complete confidence of officers and men alike & led us through the battles together with a complete courage and lack of fear that soon became an inspiration to us all.'

There was a long letter from another DCLI friend, Robin Goldsmith, by then risen to be Deputy Commander of 1st Allied Airborne Army. He had known George as the CO of 4DCLI – where:

'... I realised what a born leader he was; all his interests were in the men under his command; but above that he set a very high level of service to us all ... While nothing can equal the measure of your loss, the loss to the Army and in particular to the Regiment to which he was so devoted is also a very heavy one, and in the years to come there will be too few people like George to help pull things together again.'

Rather to my surprise, I find that my mother did get in touch with Goldsmith once he was back at the War Office in December 1945. He helped her sort out some byzantine tax problems with my father's pay.

There was a letter from one of the FANYs (First Aid Nursing Yeomanry) who had driven him around Southern Command –

probably in one of the much-admired Humber Snipe Staff Cars. She wrote as ...

> '... one who had the most tremendous admiration for George, and everything he stood for – in those far off Salisbury days, we FANYs drove many of the Staff Officers at Southern Command, but there was never anyone quite like George. He was loved by us all, and always showed such thought and kindness to everyone of all ranks he came into contact with.'

Another FANY – wise for her years – wrote in similar terms: 'The only thing we all thought, he worked too hard and did not spare himself enough.'

Perhaps the most telling note of all came from four men of George's own Regiment, the DCLI – CSM Hicks, CSM McCabe, Cpl Nelson and Private Bayliss (who had once been George's batman). It was written on a 'Memorandum' page torn from a pocket diary and said simply: 'With Colonel Millett for 23 years & he is the DCLI's biggest loss of this war.' That I do cherish. I know it would have meant the world to my father.

The Colonel of the regiment, Charles Grant, told my mother: 'I had hoped that he would have risen high in his profession, as with his record he could not have failed to do.' No mention there that his stammer might have prevented him 'rising high'. One of the sons of George's great friend David Meynell told me some years ago that, from his own experience as a professional soldier, he was certain that had my father lived and stayed in the army, he would have become a General.

I am not sure how much it eased my mother's grief to be told that her husband was so brave. For me now, seldom brave and never brave in the way he was, that accolade means a great deal. Those quotations from the letters my mother received did, of course, come carefully wrapped with sadness and concern for my mother and her sons. But these people knew his character in fun times as well as in the most testing, most lethal times.

I know very little about what happened in Elstead over those Christmas days and the disturbed weeks that followed. I am not even sure when the news of my father's death reached my mother. I can only imagine the sense of desolation that must have overwhelmed her. In the days after the news of my father's death did its utmost to blight Christmas, she certainly showed great resilience. I have been given one small insight into those awful days. My mother had formed a two-person mutual support group with her friend Sheila. Sheila wrote to her husband – the actor Hugh Latimer who was serving in India – on 29 December. She told him she had taken their young daughter Carole to 'a small party with a Christmas tree ... she enjoyed that. It was Rita Millett's party. I thought it so wonderful of her to go on with it, but she said the children mustn't suffer.'

But by the time of the memorial service for my father in the parish church, the size of the problem facing her must have overwhelmed her. The local newspaper reported: 'Mrs C.G. Millett was prevented by indisposition from being present'. My mother made a lot of use of the phrase 'hurt feelings'. I believe her own feelings were irretrievably hurt by the death of her George.

I have no memories of the longer family disturbance that followed the news that my father had been killed. The evidence I have shows that my mother wanted to draw a line and move on. So we saw very few of those army friends who had written. I am not even sure she discussed my father with Mr Lamb, the former KSLI soldier who lived nearby. I do remember one day some years later, when I was about nine, walking along the village street and noticing Mr Lamb at work, pricking out seedlings in his vegetable garden behind the pub. He unbent himself, took off his floppy, domed fedora, peered at me over the low wall and asked how I was. I nodded and said: 'Yes, okay thank you'. Then he said 'All so sad, so very sad' – and went back to his seedlings. If I had not been so stammeringly shy, I could have asked him to tell me about my father – the man he had known and I had not.

———————————

I have recently learned that Private Arnell had been married in January 1944 to twenty-year-old Rosina Sweeney who lived in Tottenham and worked in 'sugar confectionary'. A marriage that had not even lasted a whole year. As we can tell from his gravestone in the Venray cemetery, she was known to her husband as Rose. It is a desperate truth that the more you find out about individuals caught up in war, the sadder the tales you find of personal loss and the brutal disruption of home life: causing turmoil in families, liquidating present hopes and expectations and obliterating plans for the future.

———————————

It worries me greatly that I have no first-hand evidence of how my father's stammer was perceived by his fellow officers and his superiors. Those were very different times. Throughout the nineteenth century stammering had been seen as a nervous condition – and stammerers tended to be seen as nervous weaklings. It is not easy to imagine your way back into the early part of the twentieth century and gauge how stammerers and their stammers were viewed. Our focus is so fixed on continual progress from generation to generation that we are quite liable to think the worst of bygone attitudes towards any disability. We can, however, call in evidence an extraordinary quotation from the noted scientist and socialist Professor JBS Haldane. In his essay titled provocatively *Is History a Fraud?* (1932), Haldane was critical of the history then being taught in schools. He called instead for detailed studies that reveal the psychology of leaders and of crowds. He gave this example:

'Far more light is thrown on the English civil war by the fact that Charles I was afflicted with severe stammering in his youth than by the quaint legal arguments which he used to justify his ill-considered actions.'

Haldane's slight on Charles' character – based on the fact that as a youth he had 'severe' problems with his speech – is somewhat opaque. And probably intentionally so. One thing we can be clear about: Haldane believed Charles' stammer made him unsuited to be king. It meant he did not have the required qualities for leadership and could not argue his corner well enough. Because of his stammer, Haldane is saying, Charles was certainly not a man fit to navigate the turmoil of his time. It is clear he thought it perfectly acceptable to imply (if not to state openly) that stammerers are weak-willed people, probably slow-witted or even dim-witted. If that was a view held quite comfortably and generally in the 1930s and 1940s, I can only marvel at my father's ability to flourish in such a public profession as the British army. Furthermore, his ability to gain promotion despite the views many people would have had of his 'disability', leaves me in utter awe of his achievement.

The view of stammerers being intellectually impaired or of low intelligence has cropped up as late as the first decade of the twenty-first century. I had to complain very robustly when *The Guardian* – of all newspapers – published as a throwaway fact in one of its sections that stammerers are 'dim-witted'. Perhaps this writer had not heard that Isaac Newton, Charles Darwin and Alan Turing all stammered to some degree. I got swift and grovelling apologies from the writer and from his editor.

This book is not, you will have noticed, a scientific treatise. Yet it is necessary to state that current research has found no difference as regards intelligence between the brains of stammerers and non-stammerers. Indeed, there was a theory early in the twentieth century that for some people their stammer might well be caused by their superior intelligence. Only in the 1940s, did it become clear to researchers using the limited techniques and equipment then available, that there was no overall impairment of brain functions in stammerers. However, researchers using the latest scanning technology have found some 'wiring' differences in the brains of many young stammerers. These have nothing to do with levels of intelligence. They have identified some missing neural connections that may be key to creating a stammer. Further studies have shown other similar areas of the brain that may be implicated. One science writer has summed them up:

'These studies increasingly hint that people who stammer do so because of connection faults in the speech-producing networks of their brain.' There is, however, a chicken-and-egg conundrum. The question remains as to '... whether these anomalies in the brain cause the stutter or whether "natural" dysfluencies in early childhood create anomalies in the developing brains of children who go on to stammer.' There is still much research work to be done.

PART THREE

16.

SALTS OF THE EARTH –
A HAPPIER BEGINNING

Very young grandchildren are probably the world's most photographed group of people. When they are older they are no longer required to sit still and smile for granny or grandpa's wretched camera – or mobile phone. Thomas is now a tall and confident young man, studying hard at university – he is getting on with his life in a most mature way. He is, I have to remember, a whole leafy branch below me on the family tree and, most importantly, his great grandfather's stammer and his grandfather's stammer are history – stories from very different times. Although, as 'they' continue to insist, history does still have lessons for us.

I was never very good with other people's stammering. This undoubtedly began all those Christmases ago trying not to hear King George VI's painful addresses coming from Granny's wireless. Partly it has been a simple case of avoiding embarrassment. I am still embarrassed by stammerers just as some other people are still embarrassed by my stammer. It was also in part a matter of being forced to recognise that no two stammers are exactly the same. Sometimes this had in the distant past meant me hearing people judging between stammers. For instance, in school, teachers checking which stammer was the worst: 'He's not as bad as Johnny. So nothing too serious there.' Such off-the-cuff comparisons did make it more difficult to hear one's stammer talked about, especially among other parents or school staff. Most importantly, this kind of overheard chatter almost always failed to appreciate the serious impact my stammer had on my young life. It was often treated as though my stammer was merely an embarrassment to others.

Hearing other stammerers also made me realise that they too had good days and bad days. But those days were not a measure of a stammer's seriousness. 'Well, well', an uncle might say, 'haven't heard you stammering much today. So you've managed to get rid of it! Must make things much easier for you.' Based on a couple of hours of relatively fluent speech, that was pretty insulting rubbish. Little did he know that, as I grew up, my stammer was still making my life difficult and sometimes pretty impossible. The odd fluent hours were as nothing compared to my attempts to use the telephone, my failure to speak in public and the irksome level of everyday stammering.

During the first years of the new century there had been a great change in the openness about disabilities in general and stammering in particular. Complicating this have been the stark differences between types of stammer – no two people are affected in exactly the same way. This was especially true of people 'coming out' as stammerers. One of the most high profile people to go public and tell the world that stammering was simply part of their lives was the Labour politician Ed Balls. That his public speaking was sometimes interrupted by silences was well known at Westminster. As Ed Balls tells us in his book *Speaking Out - Lessons in Life and Politics*, his father had the same problem of 'blocking', merely calling it 'The speaking problem'. With his first Cabinet post he had to take questions in the House of Commons. Every time he blocked, the Tories would shout 'Errrr' at him. He only realised what his problem was when an adviser showed him the British Stammering Association's website page about 'interiorised stammering': he had a stammer. He was 41 years old and still felt he could not talk about his problem publicly – especially now he was a Cabinet minister.

Very quietly, he found a sympathetic speech therapist and got in touch with Michael Palin, the Michael Palin Centre and Action for Stammering Children. His 'key breakthrough' came when he was launching a government DVD for teachers about stammering and heard primary school children talking bravely about their own stammers. The father of one child came up to him and called him a coward for not speaking out about his own stammer – unlike the man's son: 'Why don't you give these kids some hope and confidence that you can have a stammer and become a Cabinet minister?' 'And that was the moment,' Ed Balls writes, 'I realised I had to be open about it.'

He began to speak openly about his stammer, but never so frankly and publicly as in a radio interview in 2012 after a challenging occasion in the Commons. As Shadow Chancellor of the Exchequer, he had blocked quite badly during his response to Chancellor of the Exchequer George Osborne. He faced loud barracking and mockery from the Conservative benches and mutterings that he had not done well. So, next morning, he simply told BBC Radio 4's *Today* programme that he had had a bad stammering block: 'Everybody knows I have a stammer and sometimes my stammer gets the better of me... that's just who I am.' Ed Balls says going public in this way had been 'an agonising decision'. At first he thought he had unwisely disclosed a vulnerability: 'I was very upset. Why have I done this? Why make myself so exposed?' But he soon realised the truly positive side to being open and frank about such a disability: 'It was liberating.' Certainly, he would no longer have to hear in the Commons a fellow politician saying very loudly: 'He's supposed to be the Secretary of State and he can't even get his words out.'

I have never had to 'open up' about my stammer – because it was so blatantly obvious to everyone I came into contact with. There is, however, another part of the stammering affliction that means I probably should have been more open about my own stammer. A speech therapist has told me she uses the iceberg as an image of the deep and unseen trauma a stammer will generally generate. The little bit poking up above the water line is audible – and sometimes visible in the form of jerky movements – to one and all. It is the bit that a few people may snigger at – still. It includes the obvious blocked speech or continuing running stumbles or the hesitations or explosive stuttering. The much larger part of a stammerer's problem lies hidden well below the iceberg's waterline. That includes all the emotional trappings, fears and forebodings of a stammerer's life. It may include embarrassment, a feeling of being stigmatised, guilt, shame, as well as recurrent feelings of failure as a stammerer cannot say what he or she needs and wants to say. It is often those below the waterline factors that impose limitations – an individual level of 'glass ceilings' – on a stammerer's life. So it would undoubtedly have been better if I had been brave enough to explain to more people – including girlfriends, but especially employers – that my stammer was a problem.

About ten years ago we went to a local get-together of people from our Wiltshire hamlet. It was a very pleasant evening with lots of good food and wine. But it was a very bad evening for my stammer – probably because I was having to speak across a noisy table to people many of whom I had never met before. It had become a bit too much of a public event – my stammer preferred things to be as private as possible. At the end of the evening, as we were all walking away from the house, one of the ladies at the front of the group and who had obviously had more than enough wine, suddenly turned round and said in a very loud voice: 'And who was that man with the terrible stutter?' I felt like saying, somewhat crossly: 'It was me – have you got a problem with my stammer?' But, of course, I acted as though I had not heard her crass question. Not only a stammerer, but also hard of hearing! Alison squeezed my hand – and we walked on home.

Why has that evening stuck in my mind? Very probably because since we retired and moved away from London stresses, my stammer has been less of a problem. We have new friends some of whom have expressed surprise when told I have a stammer. I am very happy to be without such an ever-present shackle – or 'impediment'. Sporadic and isolated occasions when lack of fluency becomes burdensome – those I can cope with and frequently can simply ignore. Things were getting better for me.

———————

During the years I spent working as a journalist in television, the biggest breaking news events hit me first with an overwhelming sense of inadequacy, even of futility, followed by a huge adrenalin surge. As an adult I had never experienced a body blow of personal news until, after I had retired from full-time work, some truly appalling news began seeping into our lives. It made me very angry and left me totally helpless. This was soon followed by a deep sense of guilt – obviously quite useless guilt.

Our elder grandson, the astute, the bright-as-bright, charming and always interested Thomas – then rising five – had developed a stammer.

Taking into account the impact my stammer has had on my life, especially on my early life, it should not be too hard to imagine how ghastly I felt, how my mind filled with foreboding about his future. It is one thing to acknowledge that old American research statistic that forty per cent of stammers are inherited, and quite another to discover that some rogue gene is affecting three generations within your own family: my father, myself and now our grandson. Whether there was – or needs to be – a common trigger for these genes to do their worst, we will never know. Fortunately, our two daughters did not inherit the mix of genes and happenstance that might have caused them to stammer. As we have seen, the odds on young girls developing a stammer were 4:1 in their favour. The story of this rogue gene's relationship with my brother's two sons is not so simple. It skipped safely over the younger son. But with the elder son the gene had what might be described as an unpleasant near-miss, but not a scarring near-miss. Soon after he first went to boarding school he developed a stammer.

When Peter told me about this he called it 'a bit of stammer'. But it was obvious enough to put him in the firing line of schoolboy ridicule and nasty nicknames. This is something I have only learned about very recently. Or perhaps I knew about it at the time and had – conveniently – wiped it from my memory. It is important to recall that this was still an era in which stammers were not talked about – even within families. We are talking about the mid-1970s. Had I remembered about Peter's early stammer, I might have been better prepared for the news about Thomas.

Perhaps in another memory shift (possibly also convenient), Peter is unsure how bad his stammer was. Now in his fifties, he told me: 'I do remember stammering at school. My unreliable memory tells me it would come and go.' After living abroad, his introduction to life in England was swift immersion in boarding school – the same school that his father and I had been at. Peter is still quite blunt and firm about the effects of being sent straight to boarding school:

> 'My first year boarding at Aldro was traumatic and much of it is deeply buried and inaccessible. I sobbed my way through the year and stammered in those social contexts where the light would be turned on me and required any kind of extemporary utterance – I had no problem reading prepared texts.'

Like me, Peter would get stuck on the opening 'm' of his surname – often a desperately awkward and public occurrence. Many initial consonants were also difficult: 'I do vaguely remember being teased on the lines of ovine bleats – 'baaaaaaaaaa'.' After his first year at the school, his nickname changed from 'Lamb' to 'Sheep': 'I do feel I "outgrew" getting stuck on individual sounds. I don't recall having had any issue in my last years at Aldro.' He describes his encounter with stammering as brief and negligible in comparison with other family members. He is not sure how connected his experience was to a hereditary gene. My amateur scientific view is that he had indeed suffered a trauma significant enough to trigger the gene to develop his stammer. Fortunately he had grown out of this stammer very quickly. So we are still left with the family's three stammering generations. That is something of a relief.

But why Thomas? Why our grandson? Thomas was not just extremely bright and friendly, he was, from a very early age, inquisitive and full of theories about his surroundings. He drew really well in an intuitive way. Perhaps he inherited that skill from his great-grandfather. My father was for ever making small pencil sketches – sometimes to accompany letters home. On one of his sea voyages to India he sketched a whole deck full of fellow passengers. Thomas created many pages of tiny cartoon drawings with spiky captions. These off-the-cuff creations provided him – and the rest of his family – with a great deal of fun and pleasure. He liked music and was able without any prompting to identify instruments in an orchestral piece of classical music. Like most small boys he could have spells of frustration. But for him this frustration was made worse once he started to stammer. Then one by one, drawing and music and other interests dropped away and he became fixated on wildlife – especially wildlife programmes on television. He was very keen on the programmes of Australian conservationist Steve Irwin and British naturalist Steve Backshall with his *Deadly 60* programmes. He wrote a letter of appreciation to Sir David Attenborough (almost certainly his first proper letter) and received a handwritten and very inspiring reply. Following his father's lifelong interest in ornithology, Thomas soon became very focused on birds – with a specialist's interest in birds of prey and nightjars. Over many years, his parents supported him fully in his successful training to qualify as a fully registered bird ringer.

In those first months of his stammering, Alison was as worried as I was about Thomas – and, as ever, understanding about the way it had hit me. I cried a lot and got very cross. I was cross with the world, cross with my genes and their consequences, and cross with the state of the public services that should help him. The fraught question that would never be easily answered was this: how/where could his stammer be treated and treated with a great deal more thoughtfulness and science than had been the case with my stammer?

I should not have been so hasty. Thomas has ace parents – our daughter Susannah and David. Simply brilliant parents. They were not going to let this stammer continue on its restrictive way. They contacted Sue, a long-standing friend and a one-time near neighbour of ours. She has known Susannah almost from birth. Sue trained and worked as a speech therapist. It was through Sue that Susannah and David found a really committed and far-seeing NHS speech therapist.

Carolyn Wright has been speech therapist for many years in south-west London. In the year that Thomas had his twentieth birthday, I asked Carolyn how bad his stammer had been when she first met him. She remembered clearly that she found Thomas had 'quite a significant stammer'. She is certain it was based on a 'genetic predisposition'. So what, I asked Carolyn, had triggered Thomas' predisposition? There was a lengthy pause. Then she said:

'That's difficult to be precise about. His mum said he was an early talker and from early on often had patches of being a little bit less than fluent. I think it was simply that he had excellent language skills – very obviously he was a bright little boy. He had very rich language and was very determined to talk about everything that interested him – and he was interested in so much! He was such an enthusiastic talker and wanted to find out about the whole encyclopaedia of information! He had so much to say – his whole system was wired to talk. And, in his hurry to talk and ask, he kept tripping himself up.'

It was as though his speech could not keep pace with his mind. Is this a common trigger to bring a stammer to the surface? Carolyn says that there are everyday triggers beside the more obvious traumas like car accidents or a death in the family. These less apparent triggers could include the arrival of a new baby or separation from parents and home, perhaps the shock of starting at a first nursery. Between the ages of two-and-a-half and eight, such low-key events and situations can produce a sudden non-fluency in normal, everyday speech. With Thomas it was a bit different. When this very chatty and obviously bright young chap found his chatterings and questionings got difficult, overtaking each other in his rush to make himself understood, he did become very frustrated. Frustrations I knew only too well – and with which I could sympathise. But such frustrations do nothing whatsoever to bring fluency to a child's speech.

When I was still at the sad and cross stage about Thomas – the 'Why him?' stage – and not trusting myself to talk about his stammer without collapsing into tears, I wrote to Susannah and David. She replied with a letter chock full of caring, hope and love. I shall quote a few sentences from Susannah's long and wonderful letter (14 January 2008):

'Carolyn has said that she doesn't feel we are dealing with a severe stammer. So although his speech at the moment is very bumpy (not as bad as when it first happened in April [2007] though) she feels that factors such as excitement, tiredness, over stimulation are all playing a part. And the more I listen to him speaking, the more obvious it becomes that when he has an idea he wants to express which is quickly followed by another, or when he feels he is not being listened to, the more bumpy it gets. This morning, for example, was incredibly smooth until he had so much to say in one go! We have confidence in Carolyn and the technique she is using and we will keep on keeping on! And on – until we get somewhere.'

I cannot quote much more of this letter, it is too personal. Susannah showed clearly that she understood the challenges I had faced because of my stammer. For me this was a good sign. She was open to talking about it. A real advance on bottling it up and brooding on it. She and David knew something had to be done if Thomas was not to be continually encumbered with his stammer. Here's a taste of these parents' super-mature and positive thinking – squeezed into two careful sentences:

'We want you to be happy and to enjoy this time that you've earned – don't be sad – it may go away and it may

not but we can't change that. Dave and I agree that we need
to remember that we have a very bright and kind little boy
who is healthy and happy.'

Over several years, Carolyn did Thomas a huge amount of good.
She was obviously completely in tune both with him and with his
kind of stammer. We were all introduced to the world of 'bumpy
speech' and held tight to our belief in her eventual success. Carolyn
allowed me to sit in on one of her sessions with Thomas and I was
mightily impressed. In addition to the statistic that has stuck in
my mind – my 'forty per cent of stammers are inherited' which
new research has raised to fifty per cent – Carolyn has explained
to me some more detailed statistics about young children. Five
per cent of younger children go through a phase of 'non-fluency'
– to varying degrees of severity. About two per cent grow out
of it – quite naturally. Between two or three per cent of young
children need a little help to get over that phase. Or perhaps that
should read '… ought to receive a little help …'. In just one per
cent of younger children that phase of non-fluency embeds itself
and becomes a fixed stammer – with varying degrees of severity.

In some of her sessions with Thomas, Carolyn made use of an
Australian programme of behavioural treatment for helping young
stammerers under six years old – the Lidcombe Programme. It is
most often used to train a parent so they can apply its principles
at home during normal family life. It relies on the parent giving
the child feedback – commenting directly and openly on his or her
speech. These comments should be mainly positive – commenting
on the good, fluent, smooth speech and only occasionally referring
to the 'bumpy speech'. As Carolyn emphasised, comments about a

patch of bumpy speech need to be followed by a positive 'Let's fix that'. Commenting like this does not happen throughout the day, but at specific, chosen times of the day. The parent will also measure the severity of their child stammering on a 1–9 scale so they can discuss the effectiveness of the treatment with the therapist.

Another of Carolyn's strategies was to slow things down. This was a much more sophisticated approach compared to the endless insistence that I should just relax. Thomas was talking too much, jumping in too quickly and haphazardly. One cause of his bumpiness was the way he tended to talk over other people – all part of his desire to have his say instantly. The word 'blurt' springs to mind. As soon as a thought occurred to him – and they were obviously occurring with surprising frequency – he would try to blurt out his thought or a consequent question, and in the process his words become decidedly sticky and his speech bumpy. So Carolyn introduced him to 'turn taking'. If he wanted people to listen to him, she explained that he must wait for a gap in conversation, wait his turn: 'Good waiting leads to good listening'. She made 'turn taking' into a game – and successfully instilled in him that taking turns is not just polite, but essential if you want your words to be heard and understood. And, most importantly, 'turn taking' helped slow down his speech which in turn removed more of the bumps. When I spoke to Carolyn to ask her about her therapy with Thomas, she told me she had met Thomas again recently: 'He's perfectly good at taking turns now!'

During the primary school years, Carolyn carried on with techniques to increase Thomas' fluency. She also altered the focus to include ways to ensure his confidence and self-esteem stayed high and to encourage his acceptance that it was 'okay to stammer', and also acknowledge that he had a stammer. As Thomas approached the move from junior to secondary school, worries about his speech increased. But Carolyn had an ace up her sleeve. She was able to find much sought-after places for Thomas (then ten) and his parents on one of the Michael Palin Centre's Parent Child Interaction courses. Carolyn knew all about this centre of excellence that specialised in helping young stammerers. The charity ran unique and very intensive courses. This therapy relied to a great extent on commitment by the whole family:

'When people go to the Michael Palin Centre it opens up so much. They're learning from other parents – they all help each other. Supporting parents can make all the difference – they're helped to come to terms with their child's stammer and to allay their fears about the future.'

But, Carolyn added, places on their courses are 'like gold dust'.

Susannah and David have told me how effective Carolyn was with Thomas' stammer during the years leading up to the family course at the Michael Palin Centre. They will be eternally grateful that Carolyn introduced them to the Michael Palin Centre:

'... Without the help and support of Thomas's NHS speech therapist we would not have even known about the Palin Centre course – nor I suspect would we be where we are today. From a very early age she gave him techniques to use and things to practice. She was a listening ear when things were tough and her encouragement was invaluable.'

A year after *The King's Speech* raised awareness of stammering through the story of King George VI's stammer and his speech therapist, came a BBC television programme called *The Kid's Speech*. This followed three families as they and their three stammering children attended one of the Michael Palin Centre's immersive courses. For me it was tough, emotional viewing. We watched the anguish of the three youngsters – Bethan, William and Reggie – and their parents as they were put through their paces and came to understand what stammering was and how it could be controlled. The programme was interspersed with explanatory commentary from Michael Palin. It may have been a struggle to watch, but in the end it was immensely uplifting – especially seeing the friendly commitment of the Centre's expert therapists.

The Michael Palin Centre works with and is supported by the charity Action for Stammering Children (ASC). Thomas has served on ASC's Youth Panel and his father, David, is an ASC Trustee and the charity's Treasurer. ASC has been working with the Michael Palin Centre, sponsoring research into stammering and fundraising for thirty years. During that time they have helped 88,000 children and young people from across the United Kingdom. The charity has raised over £11 million to enable this work and research to flourish and continue. Michael Palin became closely involved in the years following his portrayal of a stammerer in the popular comedy film *A Fish Called Wanda*. It was a very popular film, but, unsurprisingly, I did not find it comfortable viewing. Palin based the character on his father's stammer. He says it was '... a very serious stammer that made him cross and cantankerous much of the time'. In his father's memory, he supports the charity and the Michael Palin Centre in London.

The Centre carries Michael Palin's name and has had the support of the Ronson family (whose daughter Hayley had a severe stammer), Ed Balls (who met Thomas at the Centre), Colin Firth (who acted the part of King George VI in *The King's Speech*), Samira Ahmed (the journalist and broadcaster whose son stammered) – and many other people. Together ASC and the Michael Palin Centre work closely with the NHS and they support research into dysfluency. As a charity they have had strong support – especially financially – from the USA's Stuttering Foundation. Through an extensive public awareness campaign, this Foundation reaches millions each year with the message that stutterers can find help.

Thomas was brave about his stammer, but he was also fortunate. Many young children with stammers do not find the right therapy, let alone at the right time. That is true in Britain and around the world. And it's a big world of stammering. A recent worldwide estimate put the total number of those with some kind of stammer at 'roughly seventy million'.

A report published by ASC was titled *Suffering in Silence: Access to specialist services for children who stammer* (November 2019). Their canvass of local authorities across the UK revealed a worrying '... postcode lottery in the level of support that children who stammer receive.' They found that only forty-five per cent of health providers offered a specialist stammering service. They revealed that the access for stammering children was not just uneven across the nations, but that demand was likely to outweigh the specialist services provided by speech and language therapists. *[In NHS jargon they are SLTs. But I like to call them SALTs – just to underline their vital role in children's lives.]*

As stated in the ASC report, in 2019 there were

'... just 16,637 SLTs registered across the UK compared to 39,886 Occupational Therapists and 55,671 Physiotherapists. Approximately sixty per cent of SLTs work with children, and consequently the proportion of registered SLTs available to work with children and young people who stammer falls to 9,982.'

Some ninety-seven per cent of those therapists are women – which means the total available workforce will inevitably and understandably be reduced further by part-time working and maternity leave. Others will be working in management and research – further diminishing the number working, as we say now, on the front line. I have also been told that more SALTs are needed to help the increasing number of adult patients who, thanks to the NHS, are surviving strokes. Many stroke survivors require time-consuming help to restore their speech as they recover.

Amongst the five policy recommendations this ASC report put forward two stood out for me. Early intervention should be prioritised and there should be a national awareness raising campaign. We shall never know how many young children fail to get proper therapy and simply struggle on into restricted adulthood. Almost certainly unnecessarily.

The United Kingdom is so short of SALTs that in October 2019 they were added to the government's Shortage Occupation List. Yes, they are now categorised as 'SOLs'. This means qualified SALTs from overseas can get special, easier entry visas to work in Britain. Though how they will fare under the government's new, post-Brexit immigration process only time will tell.

I have largely forgotten how various speech therapists during my childhood approached my stammer. Now, from Thomas' parents, we have first-hand   testimony of their intensive two-week immersion course at the Michael Palin Centre:

> 'Intensive is not an overstatement – this was challenging for all of us and put us outside our comfort zones! But for all of us I think it was a sea change. Thomas was with other stammerers his own age – a first! And talking with other stammerers. He was surrounded by lovely speech therapists who gave him tools, techniques and strategies to help manage his stammer. We learnt how to manage our anxiety over Thomas's speech and how best to help him. It was tough going at times for all of us, but so worth it.'

The course was a challenge for the whole family. Thomas' younger brother Joe (then aged eight) attended the course for a day. As his mum said: 'That was a big ask for a small boy.' It was part of the course's great strength that all close family members are involved – to ensure the stammer is an open part of all their lives. There is no doubt it is a tough course. In front of others on the course, parents are invited to own up to some of their private fears about their child's stammer and how they normally react to it. This can lead to some tricky moments as realities are faced. It cannot ever be easy to keep calm and level-headed about a disability that may make your child's life ... what? A real life nightmare? A struggle? The problem often is that parents just cannot look into the future with any degree of equanimity. Stammering and equanimity do not fit tidily together. Parents are shown how trying to ignore a stammer can have a distinctly deleterious consequences. For instance it may encourage children to feel ashamed of their stammer. This course teaches children – and, vitally, their parents too – that a stammer is just part of who they are. It can be talked about just as parents can talk about other attributes of their children – hair colour or musical ability and so on.

During the course the young stammerers are pushed pretty hard. Towards the end they must leave the calm of the Centre's therapy rooms and go out into nearby streets and, with specific tasks to accomplish, talk to shopkeepers and passers-by. It is almost the equivalent of young would-be swimmers being dropped into the deep end. Before they are sent out into the deep-end of real life situations, these would-be non-stammering youngsters are well armed with techniques to help them overcome setbacks as their stammers insist on interrupting their progress towards fluency. Aged ten or eleven, I would have found this deep-end therapy very daunting. I might well have refused to do it. But armed with the techniques they have been taught on the course and practised in the safety of the Centre, nearly all of the children successfully undertake the talking tasks they have been given. There are occasionally families and youngsters that do not make it – sometimes for intrinsic reasons of family organisation that are far removed from the course itself.

For Thomas the course certainly worked, as he told me:

'The course was immensely helpful, both for myself and for my family. It was certainly challenging, but there was so much support in place, allowing me to venture outside my comfort zone, knowing that I had the help and support to do so. This, as well as the many techniques and strategies I was introduced to, taught me new methods for controlling my stammer as well as giving me new confidence and allowing me to see my stammer in a different light.'

'Another aspect that shouldn't be underestimated is simply meeting other young people with a stammer. Up to that point, I had never met anyone else my age with a stammer, and I think that meeting, interacting with and being able to relate to a group of people like me had a big positive impact on my confidence, especially at that young age.'

'I feel it also came at the perfect time for me. I was just about to make the jump to secondary school and it really helped to have that extra confidence, security and set of techniques up my sleeve before making the transition to a new school. It was an excellent boost into my teenage years, and definitely set me up very well for the years ahead.'

We can get a measure of the way the Michael Palin Centre course boosted Thomas' self-confidence and his view of his own stammer from a story his secondary school form tutor mentioned to his parents. A few terms after he arrived at the school, his tutor told Thomas that another boy with a stammer had just joined. He suggested Thomas might like to have a chat with him and tell him how he was getting on at the school. 'It's all right,' replied Thomas. 'Thank you for letting me know, but I've already talked to him. It's all fine. He'll be fine – like I am.'

This course takes a truly holistic view of stammering. Thomas' parents felt it had set him up well for his change of school:

'For us the most important things Thomas got from

the course are an acceptance and understanding that his stammer is just part of who he is and the confidence to talk about his stammer. When he started secondary school we had a meeting with his form tutor and Thomas explained the situations he found tricky. He also made the decision to tell his form group about his stammer – it took any awkwardness away and normalised it. He has done the same at university.'

'There have been tricky times since the course – stammers are very up and down – but as Thomas has matured and used all his methods, things have evened out and it just is what it is. Thomas owns it and we are incredibly proud of that.'

From my own, very concerned outsider's view – it was plain the course gave a vital boost to Thomas' self-confidence regarding his ability and willingness to speak to people outside the circle of his family and school mates. He had been lucky to find two schools which took his stammer in their stride. They made sure, for instance, that he got extra time for his language oral exams – unlike his grandfather, he has very good Spanish. He can now control his stammer. But as important is the fact that his stammer is no longer an everyday worry for him.

There are many good news stories about stammering that can raise awareness and raise the hopes of parents and their children, encouraging them to find the right therapy to help them control their stammers. When I was writing these pages during the 2020 COVID-19 lockdown I learnt of the death in Minnesota from complications with coronavirus of Annie Glenn. She was aged 100.

Annie was the wife of John Glenn, the astronaut who was the first American to orbit the earth. He became a US Senator in 1974.

Annie had a very severe stammer and had suffered many years of enforced silence. At the time her husband became a household name and was called on to make innumerable public appearances, she was unable to speak to the very persistent press – instead their children would talk to reporters. As Annie put it: 'I could never get through a whole sentence. Sometimes I would open my mouth and nothing would come out.' She was criticised in the press for being cold and offhand. She was snubbed and belittled. People would ignore her – embarrassed by her stammer or thinking she had a mental condition.

When John Glenn became a Senator, Annie took a course of therapy, which was remarkably successful. At first, her speech was noticeably slow, but she was soon making public speeches. She used her new freedom to speak passionately about stammering and the need for therapy and brought attention to disabilities of all kinds. How did she feel once she could take an active, vocal part in her husband's political campaigning and speak up for stammerers and all forms of disability? She said she felt '... like a bird being let out of a cage.'

I regret that until now I have not made more effort to support and champion stammerers. Annie Glenn puts me to shame. I even shied away from joining the British Stammering Association – now rebranded as STAMMA – let alone getting involved in its work.

The new openness about stammering is an all-round good thing. Carolyn Wright says it is 'absolutely' a positive thing. It can help relieve stammerers feeling their stammer is a burden they have to carry around with them. It is closely tied into young people owning their own stammers and accepting it as just another part of their life. In turn, for non-stammering others – like parents, friends, partners, soon-to-be partners, first dates, teachers, other relations and everyday contacts – it means acceptance that a stammer is not a stigma, does not imply any mental dysfunction or intellectual inadequacy. Carolyn also points out this openness and acceptance can pose a tricky paradox for therapists. They are helping youngsters accept that it is perfectly all right to have a stammer. However, at the same time therapists assure youngsters they can develop ways to speak with greater ease and ways to stay calm when they do stammer. That apparent paradox presents a couple of very narrow paths to tread. But in this instance there is no dilemma. There is no path not taken: both paths need to be taken. Therapists do have to tread carefully. It will take no time at all for a stammering young person to spot this paradox. After all, to repeat it just once more, stammerers are perfectly capable people. That last statement is one that is certainly no longer challenged in the daily discourse or in newspapers and broadcasts. However, we still need to be watchful.

It was the radical change in attitudes towards disabilities – including stammering – that made the most startling difference between Thomas' experience of school and the experience of my first boarding school. Those mortifying poetry recital competitions I suffered at school were as close to torture as so-called 'character building' gets. Thomas' family felt the need to make sure he did not go through similar trials. Carolyn was able to write to his school and explain what he would find difficult and how best to circumvent the problems he might face. His parents went to see members of staff to talk about his stammer. In providing five years of proportionate support, the school and particularly his teachers, played an absolute blinder. He was, for instance, given time to tell his classes about his stammer, as well as getting extra time for oral practise and exams. With my indelible memories of the way my school days were disfigured by problems with my stammer, I was delighted to see that times really had changed and the school's attitude to Thomas' stammer was exemplary. Fair and open and not at all nannying. And now, at university, he is so open about his own stammer that he can himself arrange (with the help of a letter from Carolyn) extra minutes for a timed presentation he had to make as part of his exams.

The recent movement easing stammering away from its long-term status as an ill-kept and very often somewhat shameful secret, has now gone beyond the quest for openness. Stammering is being allied to the social model of disability, seeing stammerers as disadvantaged by society's barriers rather than by their impairment. With disability campaigners this was the heart of the successful clamour for 'rights for the disabled'. Such rights are now enshrined in law in many parts of the world. This newer alliance sees stammerers as people with rights to speak as they want – or as they can. So in November 2021 STAMMA circulated a petition calling for people with stammers to appear regularly on radio and television in the United Kingdom. I dithered. Then, just a little reluctantly, I added my name. I was conflicted. I am, of course, all for stammerers having every possible opportunity to flourish as they wish and where their talents can take them. But I am still strongly connected to that young child hiding in embarrassment behind the sofa trying *not* to hear King George's – too painful for me – Christmas message.

As 2020's lockdown summer was ending, another good news story about a stammerer – again from the USA – gave me reason for a hopeful smile. A young chap with a stammer gave a two-minute address to the Democratic Party's virtual election year convention. Previously, thirteen-year-old Brayden Harrington had met Joe Biden at a rally in New Hampshire. Biden had a stammer which with a lot of practice reading, he learned to control. Even now, however, his stammer still trips in occasionally and can be heard. Candidate Biden chatted with Brayden telling him: 'Don't let it define you.' Biden explained how he continued to help stammerers and said he would help Brayden too. He was as good as his word.

Brayden's two-minute address was seen across the nation. He got stuck three times and just kept going. In the words of the revered former CBS journalist, Dan Rather, it was 'Pure, unvarnished, courage.' Now the three million or so people in the USA who stammer have a President who knows all about the embarrassment and limitations it can cause.

Among recent good news stammering stories in Britain has been the case of chronic stammerer Musharaf Asghar – known affectionately as 'Mushy'. He first came to notice in Channel 4's *Educating Yorkshire* series (2013) during which he was helped by his amazing teacher, Mr Burton. In its final episode Mushy read aloud a poem – helped by headphones that were playing music (shades of the Edinburgh Masker). A moving moment, but not, of course, a permanent answer to his problem. Channel 4 kept with him when a year later they broadcast *Stammer School: Musharaf Finds His Voice* which took him, aged seventeen, to a residential course in Guildford. This was four days of therapy for stammerers under the McGuire Programme. In Holland in 1994, David McGuire found a way out of his severe stammer using a method of breathing familiar to many opera singers (does that ring a bell?) and a traditional psychological approach known as 'non-avoidance'. His programme of therapy has since spread around the world. (I have concentrated on the Michael Palin Centre because that is where Thomas found such great support. As they say on the BBC, other brands are available.)

Sure enough, this television series began with Mushy unable to say his name when registering at a hotel. A mixture of controlled breathing and confidence building measures did allow Mushy to find his voice. But he realised it was not a full 'cure'. Sometime after the course, he cancelled a phone interview with a reporter from the *Daily Telegraph*, eventually emailing her: 'Stammer School has helped me a lot. It's giving me the chance not to overcome my stammer but to control it ... If I could speak fluently, I would show people who I really am.' I just hope he is now fluent enough to fulfil his ambition to become a teacher.

Another welcome view into the lives of a stammerer came in March 2021 with a BBC television documentary: *I Can't Say My Name: Stammering in the Spotlight*. BBC news broadcast journalist and producer Felicity Baker had spent her life trying to hide her stammer. One of her trip letters is the explosive opening 'b' of her surname. In the documentary she spoke to her BBC news colleague Sophie Raworth: 'I worked with Felicity Baker loads last year. One day she mentioned she had a stammer. I had no idea. She never spoke about it publicly.' While they were making the documentary Felicity voiced a report for BBC One news bulletins about Biden's stammer and what his Presidency could mean for young stammerers. Sophie's reaction mirrored my own: 'I think she is brave and brilliant. Huge respect.' The impact of Felicity's programme did not end there. In June 2021 the BBC launched a Stammering Support Network to help every member of its staff who stammers. This follows the successful introduction of support networks in the NHS, Civil Service and Armed Forces. That was a form of support never available to my father during his years of overcoming his 'impediment'. We are led to believe that politics and religion have always been forbidden subjects of conversation in the Officers' Mess. I suspect in his day discussion of stammering was similarly silenced.

We can now raise at least two cheers for the demonstrable fact that things are getting better for stammerers – especially as regards openness and acceptance. Getting better but not nearly as fast and as fully as they should be. As a stammerer, my father knew only too well how a lack of fluency in speech affected people's lives. In his wartime letters he wrote of getting early treatment for my stammer: '... I am sure there's a chance of nipping it in the bud.' There is no excuse whatsoever for denying young children with stammers the right and early therapy to help them make the most of their lives. Every young person who has been helped to overcome their stammer, as Thomas has been helped, is a good news story worth shouting about. Reflecting on their time with Thomas on the 'wonderful' Palin Parent Child Interaction Course, Susannah and David wrote to me: 'If only every stammering child could access this level of support.' And so, speaking very smoothly, we get back to the politics at the heart of this stammering problem. When will politicians take seriously the need for many more highly trained and committed Speech and Language Therapists (my 'SALTs of the earth') to ensure young people all over our country – whichever side of whichever coloured 'wall' they may live – have the right to receive the best possible therapies for their stammers? That is the big question. When will we hear an appropriately sized and funded answer?

So where are we now? Carolyn continues to help people with stammers. During the COVID-19 pandemic she had, like so many other people, to resort to working online. The good news is that it is proving an effective way to deliver speech therapy: 'It works,' Carolyn says, 'better than anyone hoped it could do.' But, she adds with a little laugh, 'Face to face is still best!'

Grandson Thomas is at university – starting his final year of a four-year course. He is studying biological sciences – continuing his interest in birds. He is making friends. He is flourishing despite the disappointments inherent in lockdown's virtual teaching, studying at home, curtailed fieldwork and the cancellation of large parts of normal student life. He is confident enough of his speech to agree to give a presentation on his university experience to sixth formers at his old secondary school. What's more, he enjoyed the experience.

And me? My stammer has diminished in its most obvious and overt forms. I am still unable to speak in public. I still rely on Alison's excellent telephone manner. I still have a problem with saying her name – and it's still no easier to say my surname. However, I no longer mind discussing my stammer with friends. I hope this book will enable many more people to take steps along the path away from the era of my childhood when efficacious help to overcome a child's stammer was rarely available.

Thomas has the last word – with his very positive assessment of the impact the Michael Palin Centre's Parent Child Interaction course has had on his life:

'I still use many of the techniques I learnt on that course. But I think the most valuable thing it gave me was new confidence and a new way to think about my stammer. It gave me a new perspective and encouraged being open about having a stammer, and to see it as a part of who you are, rather than something to be ashamed of. I think this change of outlook was a big thing for me and it is a mindset that has stayed with me for the many years since.'

'Overall, the techniques, confidence boost and the change of perspective that the Michael Palin Centre gave me were incredibly valuable and have no doubt helped me get to where I am.'

Acknowledgements:

Many people have helped me with this book. Most of my gratitude is reserved for Alison. She has supported my project throughout its tricky birth and development – reading endless drafts. I thank her especially for this book's title – 'Dr Alison' indeed.

A multitude of thanks to our daughter Susannah, to her husband David, to Thomas and to Joseph.

Huge thanks to the Self-Publishing Partnership and Brown Dog Books - namely Douglas Walker and Frances Prior-Reeves.

I am also grateful for help and advice to Liza Millett, Andrew Millett, Peter Millett, Nicholas Millett, Edward Stourton, Carolyn Wright, Sir Trevor McDonald, the late Sir David Nicholas, Carole Latimer, David Thornycroft, Julia Black, Simon Welfare, Genevieve Clarke, and staff at the New Zealand Medical Association.

Thanks also to Nicky Braithwaite and Pete Davies of Marlborough Photo Services for their care in rescuing endangered photographs. And to Sophie Fisher at the Imperial War Museum.

I must mention the members of the Stichting Adoptiegraven CWGC Venray War Cemetery – volunteers who look after the 2WW cemetery and keep alive the memory of those buried there.

They have helped me with important research – special thanks to Chantal Subnel. Apologies go to them and all inhabitants of The Peel for the blunt descriptions and views recorded here about its people. Voiced in 1944, they were understandable. They make awkward reading now.

Under the 'Open Government Licence for public sector information' (*) I have used extracts from many documents held in the National Archives.

(*)   See: https://www.nationalarchives.gov.uk/doc/open-government-licence/version/3/

I was assisted also by researchers at the Soldiers of Shropshire Museum in Shrewsbury.

Most sincere thanks to Ed Balls for his Foreword. Also to Dame Jane Roberts and Ria Bernard at Action for Stammering Children. And, more broadly, to the therapists at the Michael Palin Centre. I also thank Joanna Hunter for her support.

Published sources:

Lieutenant-General Frederick Morgan, *Overture to Overlord* (1950)

Patrick Delaforce, *Monty's Ironsides – from the Normandy Beaches to Bremen with the 3rd Division* (1995)

Major EG Godfrey MC with Major-General RFK Goldsmith CB, CBE, *The History of the Duke of Cornwall's Light Infantry 1939–45* (1966)

A Korthals Altes & NKCA In't Veld, *The Forgotten Battle – Overloon and the Maas Salient 1944–45* (1984 – English language edition 1995)

Major GLY Radcliffe (assisted by Captain R Sale), *The King's Shropshire Light Infantry – History of the Second Battalion 1944–1945* (1947)

Major RR Rylands, *'W' Company 2 KSLI in Normandy* and *'W' Company in North-West Europe'* – published in instalments in *The Regimental Journal* – Volumes 15–17

JRB Moulsdale, *The King's Shropshire Light Infantry* (Famous Regiments series) (1972)

Lt Col GS Jackson & Staff, 8 Corps, *8 Corps: Normandy to the Baltic* (2006)

Hugo White, *One and All – A History of the Duke of Cornwall's Light Infantry 1702–1959* (2006)

Brigadier The Right Hon Sir John Smyth, Bt VC, MC, *Bolo*

Whistler – the Life of General Sir Lashmer Whistler GCB, KBE, DSO, DL – A Study in Leadership (1967)

DR Thorpe, *Selwyn Lloyd* (1989)

Vernon Scannell, *Argument of Kings* (1987) (This extraordinary and overlooked book has the best first hand descriptions of fighting through Normandy's bocage country that I have found.)

JBS Haldane, *The Inequality of Man* (1932, Pelican 1937)

Ed Balls, *Speaking Out* (2017 edition)

Virtues of Vulnerability – Ed Balls' radio documentary, 4 January 2020, BBC Radio 4

Action for Stammering Children, *Suffering in Silence: Access to specialist services for children who stammer* (November 2019). Available here:

https://actionforstammeringchildren.org/wp-content/uploads/2019/11/Suffering-in-Silence-Action-for-Stammering-Children-Report.pdf

Sigmund Freud, *The Psychopathology of Everyday Life* (1901 – with subsequent enlarged editions)

Stephen Black, *Mind and Body* (1969)

AA Mason, *Hypnotism for Medical and Dental Practitioners* (1960)

Principles of Treatments of Psychosomatic Disorders edited by Philip Hopkins & Heinz Wolff (1965)

David Stafford-Clark, *Psychiatry Today* (1952)

Stephen Black MRCS, LRCP, GP in Kawakawa, *Hypnosis in General Practice*, New Zealand Medical Journal, 1986: 99 10–12

Paul Ferris, *The City* (1960)

Marion Davies, *The Times We Had – Life with William Randolph Hearst* (edited by Pamela Pfau & Kenneth S Marx) (1975)

Norman Mailer, *Marilyn – a biography* (1973)

Vivian de Sola Pinto, *The City that Shone* (1969)

Adam Rutherford, *How to Argue with a Racist* (2020)